The **Twenty-First** Century City

The **Twenty-First** Century City

Resurrecting Urban America

Mayor Stephen Goldsmith

Regnery Publishing, Inc.
Washington, D.C.

Library of Congress Cataloging-in-Publication Data

Goldsmith, Stephen, 1946–
    The twenty-first century city / Stephen Goldsmith.
    Includes index.
    ISBN 0–89526–435–8 (acid-free paper)
    1. Urban policy—Indiana—Indianapolis. 2. Community development, Urban—Indiana—Indianapolis. 3. City planning—Indiana—Indianapolis. 4. Indianapolis (Ind.)—Social policy. 5. Indianapolis (Ind.)—Economic policy. 6. Indianapolis (Ind.)—Politics and government. I. Title.
HN80.I54G65 1997
307.76'09772'52—dc21   97–30558
                                                                           CIP

Published in the United States by Regnery Publishing, Inc.
An Eagle Publishing Company
One Massachusetts Avenue, NW
Washington, DC 20001

Distributed to the trade by National Book Network
4720-A Boston Way
Lanham, MD 20706

Printed on acid-free paper.
Manufactured in the United States of America

10 9 8 7 6 5 4 3 2

Books are available in quantity for promotional or premium use. Write to Director of Special Sales, Regnery Publishing, Inc., One Massachusetts Ave., NW, Washington, DC 20001, for information on discounts and terms or call (202) 216-0600.

Contents

Acknowledgements

Many people deserve thanks for their inspiration, encouragement, and hard work on this project.

My wife Margaret has patiently endured the sacrifices of public life that cause me to be late to school events, miss dinners, or leave abruptly in the middle of the night for a city crisis. She helps me keep sight of the difference between what is right and what is popular, and reminds me of the things in life that are truly important. Our children Olivia, Elizabeth, Reid, and Devereaux help me understand the fragile but hopeful nature of the future. Olivia, the youngest, sat patiently watching me work on this book, encouraging me to finish while agitating for more time to play with Dad. My parents instilled in me a basic commitment to work diligently to help improve my community.

Bold public leaders across the country provided examples with their successful innovations. Neighborhood leaders, community activists, corporate citizens, and religious leaders in Indianapolis provided inspiration with their commitment to helping their fellow citizens.

The academic opportunities afforded me by Indiana University and by the Kennedy School of Government at Harvard University gave me access to great thinkers about urban problems and management, allowing me the chance to fuse policy and practice. Several foundations and think tanks have been generous with ideas, energy, and support for our initiatives. The Ford Foundation's "Innovations in American Government" program provided invaluable funding for the dissemination of our ideas.

My work in Indianapolis, and by extension this book, have received skillful advice from John Hatfield, who has been my policy advisor at the city. John gave up much of his personal time to help produce this book. Matt Lamkin made many sections clearer with his input.

Larry Mone has established the Manhattan Institute as one of the best agents of change in urban policy today, and has been steadfast in his encouragement for this project. Richard Vigilante at Regnery Publishing has displayed great patience in helping me through my first attempt at a book.

Finally, the most important and heartfelt thanks go to the people of Indianapolis, who have given me the privilege of serving as mayor.

Chapter One

The Story of America's Cities

On October 23, 1995, the Reverend Al Sharpton stood in front of the month-old centerpiece of downtown Indianapolis, a gleaming new shopping mall and entertainment complex known as Circle Centre, and called on shoppers to boycott in protest against the oppressive city administration.

Reverend Sharpton had made the journey from New York to Indianapolis to lead a rally against a proposal to allow private companies to bid for contracts to provide public transportation. His concern was that privatization would put scores of union bus drivers out of work and cut service in poor neighborhoods.

If Indianapolis "fell," he said, then the rest of the nation was sure to follow.

The controversy surrounding the provision of public transportation in Indianapolis is a wonderful example of everything that is wrong with urban policy today: the destructive effects of federal regulation, the problems that occur when government monopolizes a service, and the growing differences between the urban poor and the leaders that claim to represent their interests.

The Story of Metro

One reason people stay poor in America today is that they do not have sufficient transportation to and from the jobs that are available outside their neighborhoods. Public transportation is inadequate in many cities, including Indianapolis.

Years ago, designing a bus service that connected people to jobs was easy. The jobs were downtown. The people were in the suburbs. Establish straight-line routes radiating out from the center of the city, and call it a day.

As jobs moved from downtown to the suburbs, bus routes were slow to adapt to the changing needs of bus riders. In 1995 if a bus rider on the northwest side of Indianapolis wanted to get to a job on the city's bustling northeast side, that rider would need to take a forty-five minute bus ride downtown, transfer, and take another forty-five minute bus ride back out to the suburbs.

Neither the marketplace nor the ballot box offered solutions for bus riders, who found that the system no longer met their needs. Most could not afford cars, and taxis were prohibitively expensive. Changing the system through political power was even more difficult. Bus riders constitute barely 2 percent of the city's population and are a politically weak minority. The transit authority, commonly called Metro, is governed by an appointed five-member board, further insulating it from political accountability.

Such is the nature of government monopolies. Instead of allowing riders to redesign the bus system by expressing their preferences in the marketplace, government forced them to rely upon an inadequate service.

Over the ten years from 1985 to 1995, ridership of the city's bus system plummeted from fifteen million passengers each year to just over nine million. Even as ridership fell, Metro's budget increased from $21.8 million to $25 million. As federal subsidies and farebox revenue declined, transportation authorities raised local taxes from $3 million to $8.5 million to support the bus service.

This is a typical response for government officials, who find raising taxes the easiest solution to any shortfall in revenue. Relatively speaking, increases in tax rates to fund public transportation are slight. Well-intentioned public officials routinely determine that important services such as public transportation are "worth" a few extra dollars per month. Tax increases are particularly easy when, like the Metro board, the officials are unelected.

So taxes went up, and poor urban residents paid more for services they were using less. Perversely, government practiced wealth redistribution in reverse, collecting increasingly high taxes from the poorest segment of the population to pay bus drivers who on average made $37,000 a year.

In January 1992 we began to change the public dialogue in Indianapolis. We focused attention on the annual tax increases by public entities such as Metro, and appointed new members to the Metro board who shared a commitment to low taxes and smaller government. The resulting property tax rate freeze marked the beginning of Metro's quest to become more efficient.

One obvious way to improve bus service and address revenue shortfalls was to sell off some of the forty-foot buses and purchase a network of smaller buses and vans that could better meet the needs of riders. Congress, however, requires local public transportation authorities to repay the federal government every time a bus is sold—and at well above its market value. Because authorities like Metro lose money on each bus sold, what would have been an attractive option was nullified by federal rules.

We also encouraged Metro to open up bus service to competitive bids from private sector providers. Private providers could shoulder the capital costs of new equipment, bring a new emphasis on customer service, and reduce costs. But again the federal government all but prohibited us from implementing an innovative solution. Section 13(c) of the Urban Mass Transit Act entitled any transit worker "negatively impacted" by competition to six years' full salary and benefits as compensation.

Taken together, these provisions successfully prevented almost any attempt to break up the government monopoly on public transportation. As is all too often the case for local governments, improving service in Indianapolis required us to find a way around a series of obstacles imposed by the federal government.

In early 1995, Metro faced additional cuts in federal operating subsidies, seriously jeopardizing its ability to operate without raising taxes or cutting service. In response, the city persuaded the Indiana General Assembly to move $5.6 million of the state's support for public transportation from Metro's budget to the city budget, where federal rules governing transit authorities would not apply. Free from the constraints of federal regulations, the city could use the money to purchase services in the competitive marketplace in ways that Metro could not. We could create a flexible network of smaller buses and vans tailored to the needs of riders.

We considered this the populist answer for Metro. Poor urban residents would no longer pay more for bad service, and riders could express their preferences through the marketplace.

Shortly after the city successfully obtained the money, havoc erupted.

As the city prepared to seek proposals from private companies, Metro submitted its budget and service plan for the year. With a

$1.6 million cut in federal operating subsidies and $5.6 million of its budget transferred to the city, the bus company announced a list of routes it would eliminate as a result of its downsizing. Private providers would pick up all these routes, and more, but Metro predictably neglected that important detail in its announcement. Although the city acted quickly to assure riders that the changes would mean more service, not less, and that no routes would be cut, widespread confusion and no small degree of panic ensued.

Not only are cities on skids, but in most cases government itself has been the grease that hastened the pace of decay.

Capitalizing on the confusion was the bus drivers' union, which conducted a massive public relations campaign to tell riders that my administration was trying to save money by cutting their bus service. Every day when riders got on the bus, the drivers were there to tell them (inaccurately) that the city's plan would mean an end to evening and weekend service. Some held protests outside the City-County Building and threatened boycotts and demonstrations, drawing the attention of the local media.

An outspoken local minister from an inner-city church and a small group of elected officials joined the protest. Perhaps the most interesting member of the alliance was a local environmental organization, which reasoned that cuts in bus services would mean more smog in Indianapolis.

Finally, the Reverend Al Sharpton jumped into the fray to head off a nationwide epidemic of improved bus service.

As tends to be the case in such urban dramas, it is the poorest city residents who lose the most from this common trend of tax hikes, poor service, and oppressive federal regulation. Lacking the resources to buy services in the private sector, these citizens are at the mercy of a series of government monopolies that refuse to pay attention to their wants and needs. When reform-minded public officials and government managers seek to improve these services, the federal government and a deeply entrenched bureaucracy are there to enforce the status quo.

The Indianapolis Metro story is anything but an isolated incident—it is the story of American cities for the past four decades.

Greased Skids

For two hundred years, America built great cities. People flocked to cities because they were places of limitless opportunity. Despite pockets of poverty, and even slums, many urban neighborhoods were home to vibrant civic organizations and communities of faith. The unemployed and the working poor shared their neighborhoods with large numbers of middle-class families, who provided positive role models and support for struggling neighbors. Strong families, churches, and schools worked together to instill a sense of unity and a shared set of values. Cities were where people went to pursue the American dream.

Today, the American dream for many is to escape the city for the comforts of the suburbs. Cities are losing population, and businesses increasingly locate outside city limits. Badly deteriorated inner-city neighborhoods are places of widespread unemployment and intolerably high rates of crime.

Ed Rendell, the Democratic mayor of Philadelphia, is fond of quoting a rather glum prediction by Professor Theodore Hershberg of his city's University of Pennsylvania:

> All of America's cities are on greased skids. What differentiates one from another is the angle of descent. And unless there is a major shift in public policy, America will lose all its major cities.

Hershberg was correct. Not only are cities on skids, but in most cases government itself is the grease that has hastened the pace of decay. Urban programs based on the principle of wealth redistribution trapped those who did not work in a web of dependency, inflicted poor families who did work with the highest marginal tax rates in the country, and isolated both groups in inner cities by driving out the middle class with higher taxes.

By making teen pregnancy and illegitimacy economically viable through welfare, while abdicating responsible enforcement of child support laws, government subsidized the breakup of the family, with disastrous consequences.

Ineffective urban school systems failed to equip an entire generation of youths with the skills they needed to succeed in the workplace, while at the same time preserving a monopoly that denied poor families the option to escape that is available to middle-class families. Meanwhile, forced busing destroyed the fabric of many neighborhoods, and the often accurate perception of substandard schools provided yet another reason for families to head for the suburbs.

Instead of sending strong messages to youths when they first got into trouble, a nonexistent juvenile justice system waited to deal with them until they were hardened and unreformable, to the benefit of neither society nor the individual.

Many point to the War on Poverty as the turning point. The program signaled the beginning of an era in which government would attempt to solve the problems of inner cities through massive wealth redistribution. As government attempted to buy cities out of poverty through impersonal programs, it supplanted private efforts and raised taxes in the process. Worse, while government spent billions on an ever-increasing array of social programs, it neglected its core responsibilities of public safety and infrastructure.

Excessive taxation, crumbling infrastructure, bad schools, and rising crime rates prompted an exodus of those who could afford to leave, robbing poor residents of the benefit of these strong families and weakening stabilizing institutions such as churches and neighborhood associations. This flight of wealth left a smaller, poorer tax base and caused chronic revenue shortfalls. Predictably, government's solution was to raise taxes further and pour more money into programs, and a vicious cycle began.

Jane Jacobs, in her classic *The Death and Life of Great American Cities,* understood in 1961 that the War on Poverty would fail:

> There is a wistful myth that if only we had enough money to spend—the figure is usually put at a hundred billion dollars—we could wipe out all of our slums in ten years, reverse decay in great, dull, gray belts that were yesterday's and day-before yesterday's suburbs, anchor the wandering middle class and its wandering tax money, and perhaps even solve the traffic problem.

> But look what we have built with the first several billion: low-income projects that become worse centers of delinquency, vandalism, and general social hopelessness than the slums they were supposed to replace.

The War on Poverty was rooted in the notion that government knows better than people what is in their best interests and that government must solve social problems. Big-city mayors bought into this doctrine as well, attempting to address the problems facing their cities through what Milwaukee Mayor John Norquist disdainfully calls "the pity strategy." This strategy led mayors to Washington, tin cups in hand, saying, "Pity me, we have awful problems, I need financial help." The bigger the problem, the bigger the handout, the worse the outcome.

A Smaller Government Approach

As urban problems continued to worsen, the days of simply pouring more money into failed programs inevitably came to an end. Fiscal crises forced several mayors to reexamine the way they did business, with many turning to privatization and other efficiency measures in hopes of getting more value out of fewer tax dollars. The best of these efforts produced notable successes, some of which are described in such excellent books as *Reinventing Government* by David Osborne and Ted Gaebler, and *Revolution at the Roots* by John O'Leary and Bill Eggers.

Cities can once again be the pride of the nation in the twenty-first century.

Part of what distinguishes our experience in Indianapolis from some of these other efforts is that we were not prompted to change because of a crisis. While Indianapolis has its share of big-city problems, the city also benefits from more than twenty years of enlightened corporate involvement and strong leadership by mayors Richard G. Lugar and William H. Hudnut.

When I came into office in 1992, Indianapolis's finances were sound: taxes were relatively low, our public workforce seemed lean, and the city boasted a healthy bond rating. Rather than adopting a fire-sale privatization approach, we implemented a comprehensive approach to city management based on a belief that smaller government is just plain better.

At every juncture, a few simple principles guided our decision making:

- People know better than government what is in their best interest.
- Monopolies are inefficient, and government monopolies are particularly inefficient.
- Wealth needs to be created, not redistributed.

- Government should do a few things well.
- Cities must not raise taxes or price themselves out of competition with excessive regulations.

We made mistakes, as well as our share of adversaries, in the process. As in the Metro story, we dealt with intransigent middle managers, stubborn federal bureaucrats, self-interested advocates of the status quo, distrust from residents of long-neglected neighborhoods, and other obstacles to change.

Yet we remain optimistic. From 1992 to 1997 our efforts to move city services into the competitive marketplace saved $230 million. During that period we cut the city budget each year. We did not just cut the rate of growth, we actually spent less. Our budget in 1997 was 7 percent lower than the budget when I took office. We reduced the nonpublic safety work force (everybody but police officers and firefighters) by more than 40 percent. At the same time, we made the largest infrastructure investment in the city's history—more than three-quarters of a billion dollars—and put one hundred more police officers on city streets, while reducing taxes slightly.

Today, more people are moving into Indianapolis than at any time in decades. The city has enjoyed four consecutive years of record job creation and record numbers of new homes built. Unemployment recently dropped below 3 percent, the lowest level since such statistics have been kept.

As word of our approach spread to public officials and other observers of urban policy, we quickly discovered that there was a market for our experiences. Our efforts drew hundreds of public managers to the city for seminars and tours, talented individuals who brought with them scores of additional good ideas. In 1993 I had the good fortune to meet Larry Mone, president of the Manhattan Institute, and Myron Magnet, editor of the institute's outstanding *City Journal* (probably the best source of good ideas on urban policy), who encouraged us to collect our experiences in a book, in the hope that an overview of our successes and failures and the policies that produced them might prove useful. This book is the result; it describes an approach, under way in Indianapolis, to prepare cities for the twenty-first century through an explicit policy of reducing the size of government, creating wealth through the marketplace, and rebuilding civility by giving authority back to families, churches, and neighborhood associations.

The first section of this book describes our efforts to break up government monopolies and move city services into the competitive marketplace. Chapter Two argues that governments are inefficient because they are monopolies, and describes how Indianapolis subjected government services to the rigors of free-market competition. Chapter Three describes some of the services that are now provided by private companies, and debunks the myth that the only way to reduce budgets is to cut service. Chapter Four tells the surprising story of how Indianapolis unions rose to the challenge of competition, and Chapter Five concludes with some of the management tools we developed to make government more efficient.

The next section outlines our strategies for making Indianapolis a competitive place for companies to do business, as well as for ensuring that city residents receive maximum benefit from economic growth. Chapter Six describes our small-government approach to economic development, which deemphasizes the role of tax incentives and other traditional approaches and focuses instead on cutting taxes and reducing regulations. Chapter Seven addresses the importance of a market-based delivery system for moving welfare recipients into private sector jobs, and Chapter Eight examines how the same principles of individual choice and decentralized decision making can improve public education.

Finally, the last section describes how government can play an important role in revitalizing troubled urban communities by living up to core responsibilities and supporting grassroots efforts at neighborhood renewal. Chapter Nine describes a community-based approach to public safety, and Chapter Ten discusses how to rebuild urban infrastructure and nurture effective neighborhood organizations. Chapter Eleven explores the critical role of families, churches, and other institutions that bind communities and transmit important values.

Cities can be places of opportunity and a high standard of living, as well as competitive places to do business. Despite decades of misguided policies, a handful of American cities are making comebacks, riding a wave of initiative at the grassroots. Neighborhood leaders like Olgin Williams, Violet Gwin, Carolyn Hook, and others you will meet in this book are representative of thousands more in cities across the country. They provide hope that troubled neighborhoods can succeed, and that cities can once again be the pride of the nation in the twenty-first century.

Chapter Two

Making a Market

Cities no longer compete against each other for businesses and families. They compete against their suburbs, and they are losing badly. Virtually every large, older city has lost population over the past thirty years.

Every time a family moves out, every time a business relocates, every time a new business starts up in the suburbs, the central city loses a little bit of its tax base. This creates pressure for more revenue, and increases the temptation to raise tax rates, driving more businesses and homeowners away. It is an ugly downward spiral, and cities all across the country are caught in it.

Robert Inman, professor of finance and economics at the Wharton School of Business, describes the phenomenon in bleak terms:

> The jobs and families that leave the city as taxes rise
> are likely to be the best paying jobs and the wealthier

families. The loss of high-wage firms is likely to discourage educational investments by current residents
and to deter the in-migration of good jobs and skilled
workers in the future. As the population of the city
becomes less skilled, average wages are likely to
decline, and falling incomes often create additional
pressure for local government services. Rising service
demands and falling tax bases mean more, not less,
pressure on the city's deficit.

Public officials are only now recognizing that holding the line
on taxes is more than just a campaign slogan—it is an economic
necessity. They are reacting by searching more aggressively than
ever for solutions that do not involve higher taxes.

Changes in Washington are also turning up the heat on cities.
For the past thirty years, the federal government has responded to
urban problems through expensive entitlement programs that
reimburse local governments for their costs without holding local
officials accountable for achieving results. The more poorly
administered and inefficient the effort, the greater the federal
subsidy.

The 104th Congress changed the system by giving responsibility
for many programs back to local officials and providing block
grants to pay for them. Today these local officials have greater
flexibility, but limited funds. For the first time in decades, they
must concentrate on efficiency and performance if they are to continue providing the services citizens have come to expect from
government.

Elected officials also face another, more subtle, pressure. Americans have always joked about the inefficiency of their government—witness the debate over national health care, which some
pundits observed would combine "the efficiency of the post office

with the compassion of the IRS." There is an important issue underlying these jokes. Private enterprise and government share patrons. Customers to one are taxpayers to the other.

While customers apply for bank loans at automated teller machines, taxpayers still endure painfully slow service at the license branch. Construction companies can order supplies over the Internet, but they lose time and money waiting in line for permits at City Hall. Most service

Privatization is an attempt to reverse much of the history of the twentieth century.

companies offer twenty-four–hour help lines for their customers, while government remains strictly a nine-to-five enterprise. Tenants exit neatly trimmed office parks and private subdivisions to travel along poorly maintained public rights-of-way.

Taxpayers will tolerate some level of inefficiency and unresponsiveness from government, but as taxes continue to rise, their patience wears thin. Citizens demand better value from those they elect.

These factors converge to force government officials to become better managers. Not surprisingly, many elected leaders now talk about "running government like a business," and an emerging solution for many policymakers is to turn over the delivery of many services to private sector firms.

"Privatization," as it is called, describes the process of turning over to the private sector the job of running public services that are ordinarily, and often exclusively, provided by the government. The term was coined in the mid-1970s by Robert Poole, who today runs the Reason Foundation in Los Angeles, a think tank that boasts some of the nation's best-known experts on privatization.

The idea is simple: just because government has a duty to ensure that citizens receive certain services does not necessarily dictate that government must produce those services itself.

The principle should be obvious. Our nation has decided, for instance, that it should guarantee that low-income people can obtain nutritious food. But the government does not grow food, nor for the most part does it distribute food. Through the Food Stamp program, people on public assistance can buy the same food at the supermarket that other people buy—food sold by grocery stores, packaged by private companies, and grown on private farms. Think how much simpler that is than the alternative—a huge complex of government-run farms, government processing and packing plants, and government supermarkets. It would be a disaster. In fact it was a disaster—in the Soviet Union, for one.

Yet while our government abstains from running farms and supermarkets, it does assume responsibility for directly providing many other services that are common in the private marketplace. We want every child to get a good education—so the government runs schools. We want everyone to be able to send and receive mail—so the government runs the Postal Service. We do not want garbage to pile up in the streets or let sewage spread disease—so government hauls garbage and builds water treatment plants. All of these services the government provides itself, even though all of these functions can be and many times are performed better and more cheaply by private industry.

Poole and other privatization advocates argue that the best way to keep local and state governments from going broke, while at the same time providing first-rate services, is to turn over much of what they actually do to the private sector—not only obvious functions such as collecting garbage, which is already done by private haulers in many areas, but even services we almost automatically think of as public, such as running prisons, or even collecting taxes.

"There is not a single type of service that local government is providing today that isn't privatized somewhere," says the Cato

Institute's Stephen Moore. And in most cases private vendors are more efficient than their government counterparts.

Privatization is an attempt to reverse much of the history of the twentieth century, during which the government took upon itself an astonishingly broad array of tasks—many of which it now attempts to provide almost exclusively, i.e., with as little competition from the private sector as possible.

Many of the best services in newer suburbs have been privately provided from the beginning: from trash collection and street maintenance to private security. These edge cities, born well after World War II, never had a progressive era to overcome, which meant there was no tradition of big government and no bureaucracy to fight. They had a clean slate, and the only question was how to provide the best service at the lowest cost. The answer was often found in the private sector.

Despite scattered examples of privatization in large cities, when I took office in 1992 the question remained whether privatization could work in heavily urban areas, where resources were scarce, the demand for services was great, and the bureaucracy was thoroughly entrenched.

We came into office betting that yes, it could.

Competition, Not Privatization

Fortunately, as revolutionaries go, we tended toward the button-down, Midwest, Republican variety. In order to learn how privatization really worked, we decided early on that we would start with a small, doable project that would not attract much political resistance.

One of the first services we attempted to privatize was the billing of the city's sewer users. In Indianapolis, the sewers are run by the Department of Public Works (public works). Naturally enough, public works employees mail out and collect sewer bills. Privatizing this function seemed a perfect test case for several reasons.

First, it seemed to cost too much. In 1992 the city spent nearly $3 million to collect $40 million in sewer bills.

Second, there was an obvious private partner. Sewer bills are based on the amount of water used as determined by the Indianapolis Water Company, a private utility that provides Indianapolis residents with drinking water. The water company also turns off water lines for the city when sewer users do not pay their bills. Even better, the company was preparing to open a new customer service center.

We approached the water company about taking over sewer billing. The company agreed enthusiastically, and offered to do the job for 5 percent less than our cost of $3 million.

We were disappointed. While we had committed to starting with a small project, we were hoping for more than small savings. In retrospect, however, we should not have been surprised. After all, our plan amounted to this: In the name of privatization, we were going to replace a public monopoly with a private monopoly. For that we expected to reap huge savings?

The truth is that although "privatization" seemed like a useful piece of shorthand for what we wanted to do, it was actually misleading and threw us off track. The key issue, we soon discovered, was not whether tasks were performed by public or private institutions. A private monopoly, like the water company, might be less bureaucratic and more efficient than a government monopoly. But without the spur of competition, the difference in what we could expect in price and service would be distinctly unrevolutionary.

We approached sewer billing in a different way, contacting every utility in central Indiana and asking them to compete for the sewer bill job. Forced by competition to further effort, the water company returned with a new proposal to collect sewer bills for

$2 million annually, for a savings of 30 percent—six times the amount it had offered originally.

More impressive from our perspective, IWC went a step further by offering to find unbilled or underbilled sewer users, collect the missing revenue, and share the earnings with the city. The company offered the first $500,000 in collections to the city, and proposed to split additional collections evenly. So without hiring any more employees, conducting any studies, or installing any more auditors, the city has earned savings and revenues from this small example of more than $10.6 million to date.

The city market is abundant, not austere.

Dramatically lower costs coincided with better service. Sewer and water bills now appear on one statement, so our customers have one less monthly check to write. In addition, customers have one office to call for sewer and water service and billing information. The office also stays open longer, which improves customer service.

Our experience with sewer billing made an immediate impact on our thinking about privatization. Competition, not privatization, made the difference. Competition drives private firms—and, as we soon discovered, public agencies—to constantly seek ways to reduce costs and improve service. The pressure exerted by customers and the threat of losing out to competitors are what spur innovation and overcome the natural bureaucratic resistance to change in public or private institutions.

Creating Markets

The second event that changed our thinking about privatization occurred when we decided to seek competitive bids for the maintenance of a small section of the city's streets. When our Department of Transportation workers learned that they would have to compete to keep the work, amazing things happened.

To be honest, we thought our city workers had no chance of defeating private companies in direct competition. Traditional notions of government workers as bureaucratic and even lazy led us to believe that public employees faced an uphill battle in competing with the lean, mean private sector.

Transportation workers were skeptical too, but for a very different reason. They did not think we were serious about letting them bid. They thought we were setting them up for failure. And when they insisted that we talk seriously about the problems they faced in competing with private firms, it turned out they had a point.

The workers complained they could not possibly compete while carrying unreasonable overhead in the form of managers' salaries. For a mere ninety-four workers in the street repair division there were thirty-two politically appointed supervisors—an absurd ratio, especially considering that most of the supervisors were relatively highly paid. In part to call my bluff, union employees told us that if we were serious about competition we would eliminate several of these supervisors to give the union a real chance to compete.

By normal political standards the union's demand would have been a show stopper. The supervisors were all registered Republicans. I was a Republican mayor. These managers, and their patrons in the party, had supported my election. The union had supported the opposition and campaigned strongly against me. Now the union wanted me to fire politically connected Republicans to help a Democratic union look good.

We did it. We had to. If I had blinked and shielded my fellow Republicans, the message would have been clear: we were not serious about competition. In addition to laying off or transferring fourteen of the thirty-two supervisors, we provided the workers with a consultant to help them prepare their bid.

The union was surprised, impressed, and probably nervous. Workers now knew that they, too, would be finding new jobs if they failed to draw up a competitive plan.

Making workers responsible for their own destiny sent a clear message that for the first time in ages management recognized that the men and women who do the job know better than anyone what it takes to get it done. Simply empowering these workers transformed them into efficiency experts overnight. They became incredibly creative in imagining how they could do their work more cost effectively. As Todd Durnil, the deputy administrator of street maintenance, observed, "We took the shackles off the guys. We tapped their knowledge and experience instead of telling them what to do."

For example, street repair crews previously consisted of an eight-man team that used two trucks to haul a patching device and a tar kettle. Once in charge, the city workers saw that by remounting the patching equipment they could eliminate one of the trucks, and by doing so reduce the crew from eight to five.

The city employees bid significantly below their private competitors and won the job decisively. While the city previously spent $425 per ton filling potholes with hot asphalt, the new proposal reduced the city's cost to $307 per ton—a 25 percent savings.

We were shocked. In fact, many within city government doubted the union proposal. But when DoT actually did the work, workers not only met the bid price, they beat it—by $20,000. They increased the average production of a work crew from 3.1 to 5.2 lane miles per day—a 68 percent efficiency increase.

Union leaders declared that the bidding process brought them "from darkness into daylight." Isaac Sanders, a crew leader responsible for street repair, said that before the bidding process, "we didn't give a hoot what anything cost," but because of competition "we got efficient real quick."

The pothole competition confirmed that a preoccupation with privatization is unproductive. Contrary to their poor public image, most civil servants are hardworking and talented—and they know a lot more than their mayors do about how to do their jobs well. The problem is that they have been trapped in a system that punishes initiative, ignores efficiency, and rewards big spenders.

Our experiences with sewer bills and street repair led us to adopt an explicit model of competition between private firms and public employees. From the taxpayers' point of view, the ideal situation occurs when the most efficient private sector service provider goes head-to-head with a government division operating at its most efficient level.

This new appreciation of the importance of competition shifted our focus away from privatization and toward what we began to call "marketization." For us, marketization meant creating a market where none previously existed. Today, throughout city government, we are trying to create a true market, a place where competition continually generates lower costs, better service, and new ideas for helping citizens.

Monopoly

In retrospect, the importance of marketization seems simple. Why are most private sector companies more efficient, more customer-oriented, and more innovative than government? Because private sector companies are in competition and will go out of business if customers do not like the goods and services they offer.

Government, on the other hand, has a monopoly on the delivery of a wide range of services and control over vast assets. It is not *only* a monopoly, but a particularly effective *form* of monopoly. There are four crucial ways in which government is exempted from market pressure or protects itself from competition:

The crucial factor in a free market is not fear but freedom.

No. 1. Government Cannot Go Out of Business

Government never faces the ultimate sanction faced by every business that lets down its customers. Every citizen of the United States, like it or not, is a captive customer for government services—and a new customer is born every few seconds. Poorer Americans are particularly captive, as they must rely on services such as public transportation and public schools.

No. 2. Government Controls Revenue and Can Raise Its Prices Even When Its Products Are Unpopular

If more money is needed to provide a given service, government will raise taxes to pay for it. While the private sector has to persuade people to make purchases, government simply takes dollars. General Motors would never close a plant if it could seize the assets of people who do not want to buy its cars.

No. 3. Government Can Spend More Than It Takes In

While some states and cities are technically required by law to balance their budgets, most government entities are not—including the federal government. Even governments that by law must balance their budgets avoid doing so by borrowing, deferring capital spending, and employing questionable bookkeeping devices.

Private companies, and families, can deficit spend only in the short term before going bankrupt or out of business; government thinks it can go into debt indefinitely.

No. 4. Government Delivers "Essential Services"

Whenever reform-minded managers or elected officials exert pressure to reduce costs, status-quo managers can mount an effective defense by pointing to the essential nature of their task. A call for budget cuts in a municipal Department of Public Safety, for example, might be met with a cry that the streets will be less safe. Attempting to slow the growth of education spending meets with a despairing "Aren't our kids worth a few extra dollars a month?" This strategy resonates powerfully with the people, who have neither the time nor the inclination to scour budgets to see if savings are possible without cuts in service quality.

These four characteristics of government monopolies explain why government constantly grows and why no one really expects it to perform very well. They also explain why, whatever the crisis, the answer is almost never "cut the budget."

To survive, urban governments must toss away these crutches. Only then will they be able to do what private institutions do every day—increase quality and cut costs simultaneously.

Our attempt to create a market inside government meant changing the rules. We determined to let ourselves "go out of business" in certain areas if we could purchase a better deal in the private sector. We planned to shift many of our costs from taxes to user fees, so that our customers could let us know if we were providing poor service. We declared that raising taxes would not be an option, so departments that wanted more revenue for favored programs would need to find it within their own budgets. And we began to tie all of our costs to specific performance measures, so that citizens could decide for themselves if specific services were worth their cost. This was to be our city market.

The Yellow Pages Test

Making the distinction between privatization and competition provided us with an important new understanding of how to use the marketplace to improve city services. Having made two successful forays into competitive contracting, we began to seek out other city services that could benefit from being moved into the evolving city market.

We quickly discovered that some services are more obvious candidates for competition than others, and that identifying the "low-hanging fruit" can provide governments with lucrative and relatively straightforward competitive initiatives. There are, we learned, a few basic ways to determine a given service's ripeness for competition.

It is useful, for example, to determine whether an activity requires the making of policy, or merely the implementation of policy that has already been established. Deciding which streets to repair in a given summer is a policy decision; laying the asphalt is implementation. This is similar to the distinction Osborne and Gaebler make between "steering" and "rowing" in *Reinventing Government*. We found that services that involved "rowing" were good candidates for competition.

Another issue worth addressing was whether the activity represented a core service that government must provide for citizens, or only supported the provision of these core services. We learned that support services, such as mailing sewer bills, usually had direct private sector counterparts and often resulted in privatization. Core services such as street repair, on the other hand, often resulted in successful bids by our own employees.

Our early rule of thumb was simple and is still probably the best guide. Look at the city's yellow pages. If the phone book lists three companies that provide a certain service, the city probably should not be in that business, at least not exclusively. If there are five florists in Indianapolis, the city probably does not need its own hothouse; if window-cleaning services are booming, why should the city operate its own? The best candidates for marketization are those for which a bustling competitive market already exists. Using the yellow pages test, we could take advantage of markets that had been operating for years.

Printing was a great example. Before 1993 the city spent $1.4 million annually to run three print shops and operate more than two hundred copiers.

Yet the yellow pages contained scores of private printers, entrepreneurs whose first thought in the morning and last thought at night was how to shave a hundredth of a penny off the cost of a copy. Several vendors came in with bids that would save us almost 30 percent of our cash cost.

We selected Pitney-Bowes Management Services, a vendor that would provide all our copying services, plus everything the print shops had been doing for us, for only $1 million—a savings of almost $400,000 a year, or 27 percent. But that was only the beginning. The competition for the city's business was so fierce that we were able to press for additional benefits.

Pitney-Bowes set up an in-house copy center, renting space in the basement of the City-County Building. The company established 120 pickup points throughout city offices for copy and print requests. Throughout the day, Pitney employees visit these locations on a preset schedule to pick up work and drop off finished products.

There are still 160 copy machines available in city offices for fast copies and short documents—which Pitney restocks each morning with paper and toner—but the new copy center now produces 78 percent of all of the city's copies, saving hundreds of clerical hours each year.

Finally, Pitney-Bowes generated unexpected savings when it helped us conduct a "red tape" initiative to reduce the number of forms produced by city departments.

The yellow pages test produced dramatic results. Over the years even the prudently managed city of Indianapolis had ventured far afield. The city ran golf courses, tree nurseries, and even a window-washing service. We had done these things for so long that they seemed like obvious government functions even though to an outside observer they might seem absurd. Tree nurseries?

Do what is easy. That is the first thing we learned and the first thing a city should do. The easy stuff will not turn a city around tomorrow, but it is a start. As a wise man once said, "The greatest difference in the world is the difference between somewhat better and somewhat worse."

So pick up the yellow pages. And let your fingers do the walking to better service and lower costs.

Chapter Three

Not Just Cheaper, but Better

We started by doing what seemed easy, as indicated by the yellow pages test, although not everything that passed the test was easy. We consistently showed that free-market competition could do something critical to solve the fiscal crisis facing state and local governments all over the country: it could increase service while cutting costs, thereby changing the basic equation that describes government failure everywhere today. Competition could stop the spiral of higher taxes paying for worse services.

Raising quality in the very act of reducing costs is the driving force behind most economic progress. It is a lot more expensive to travel long distances by horse and buggy than by car, even though the horse and buggy, technologically, is a simpler mode of transportation. It is cheaper to go by car than by buggy *because* of better technology—cars are faster, cleaner, safer, and more comfortable. And flying cross-country is cheaper than driving, for the same reasons.

Yet to most government managers, cutting budgets while increasing services seems impossible—a bizarre and paradoxical dream. The problem starts with campaign promises. As anyone who has ever observed a political campaign understands, candidates tend to think and speak in terms of dollars instead of results. Those who want to be viewed as tough on crime will propose spending more money on prisons; those who want to be seen as compassionate will offer more money for social programs. Consider the private sector equivalent: no CEO would last long if he promised his board of directors that he would raise costs every year.

Conversely, proposals to cut the budget are invariably met with questions about *which* services will be cut—again because "everyone knows" that government cannot cut costs without reducing service.

The notion that—by definition—more government spending improves services is the single most destructive idea that hampers government policy today. It explains why so many attempts to get federal, state, and local budgets under control start in deceit and end in gridlock. We all agree the budget must be cut, but the underlying assumption is that services must therefore be reduced, which means the debate boils down to an argument over whose ox gets gored.

In its most famous form, this budget gridlock is the Washington Monument Gambit.

Anybody who has ever discussed the difficulty of cutting government budgets knows how the gambit goes: The president asks every department to cut its budget by 10 percent, just by trimming the fat. A week later the Department of the Interior says that, sure, it can cut the budget by 10 percent, no problem. All it has to do is shut down the Washington Monument, the Grand Canyon, and, in tough years, the Lincoln Memorial. Why those things? Well, says Interior, that fun stuff is the fat. Everything else is a vital government service. Cut vital government services, and we are on the road to ruin. These indulgences have to go.

Of course, no one wants to shut down the Washington Monument. The budget cut is DOA.

By contrast it is easy to make that other side of government—the deeply entrenched bureaucracy, the invisible government that citizens barely see and rarely understand—look like the bone that cannot be cut. Cut into that real stuff, the bureaucrats say, and the schools will close, the bridges will collapse, and children will starve in the streets. And precisely because most of the bureaucracy is virtually invisible, citizens are in no position to argue.

From 1992 to 1997 we subjected more than seventy services to the rigors of free market competition. Not every marketization was a complete success, but by breaking up our monopoly, we exposed the hidden bureaucracy and showed it can be cut.

A small but dramatic example of the possibilities occurred when we addressed the problem of abandoned vehicles. Like most urban areas, Indianapolis has a problem with stolen or junked vehicles that are abandoned on public property, usually on streets in poor neighborhoods. These vehicles are not only eyesores, but also can be safety hazards for children. City inspectors respond to complaints by tagging the vehicle with a notice giving the owner seventy-two hours to move the vehicle. After seventy-two hours the car is towed to an impound lot, and after a grace period the city can dispose of the car.

In 1993 the city towed nine hundred abandoned vehicles—approximately one-tenth of the complaint calls it received from neighborhood residents. Even after selling unclaimed cars, the cost to the city was $174,000 to tow, store, and dispose of these vehicles.

In 1994 we solicited proposals from private firms for the towing and disposal of our abandoned vehicles. ADESA Auctions, a private company that knew a great deal more about selling automobiles than we did, won the contract by proposing to pay us for the right to dispose of unclaimed abandoned vehicles.

During the contract's first year, ADESA towed nearly 2,300 vehicles. Police officers tell me it was common for residents to stand on their porches and applaud when some of these vehicles were finally hauled away. In the first two years of the contract, the city earned $500,000 from the sale of abandoned vehicles while dramatically improving the service provided to neighborhood residents. Where government saw an expense, a private company found a profit—and today the removal of abandoned vehicles *earns* money for taxpayers.

The connection between better service and lower costs—or in this case, the creation of profits—was anything but accidental. Rather, it was the act of enhancing services that put the removal of abandoned vehicles in the black.

While we were gaining confidence in our new methodology, many remained suspicious of private companies providing government services. The complaint goes like this: Private companies have to make a profit, which means they must siphon dollars away from the government services they have been hired to provide, which means (here is that notion again) reducing the quality of service. Whenever possible, private companies would provide inferior services to increase profits—often by replacing relatively high-paid professional civil servants or union workers with cheap labor.

Nothing could be further from our experience. To the contrary, the competitive process allows us to specify the level of service quality vendors must provide—something we simply could not do within a government monopoly. If they do not meet our standards, we can fire them—while by contrast it is virtually impossible to get rid of even one bad public employee, much less an underperforming division. Instead, we found that private companies were able to cut costs and improve service through innovation, skilled management, creativity, and customer service. Our private partners even tended to offer higher wages and better benefits to their employees.

As anyone who has ever observed a political campaign understands, candidates tend to think and speak in terms of dollars instead of results.

The following examples explore some of the various ways that private providers were able to offer benefits for Indianapolis taxpayers.

Superior Management Expertise

Indianapolis operates two advanced wastewater treatment plants that remove impurities from the city's sewage, and release clean water into the White River. When we began to consider putting the water treatment systems up for competition in 1992, industry experts considered these plants among the best run in the country, and our employees won numerous national awards in competition against other governments.

Trying to improve the plants through competition would be our biggest challenge to date, and not merely technically. With a sensitive service such as wastewater treatment, many of our hurdles were political.

Union workers at the plants teamed up with distrustful environmental groups to vigorously oppose any private involvement. The City-County Council also offered some initial resistance. Beulah Coughenour, the Republican council member who had been responsible for the construction of the two plants, worried that private management could not possibly generate sufficient savings to justify what some considered a risk to water quality. As our review committee began to prepare a request for proposals from private vendors, Coughenour and several members of the council requested that we first hire an outside firm to conduct an efficiency audit.

We hired a Big Six accounting firm to study the plants from top to bottom and assess the potential savings from private management. The report confirmed our general belief in the efficiency of the plants, noting that the plants were among the best government wastewater plants in America. The thick report had a simple bottom line: we could expect to reduce operating costs by 5 percent.

There it was again—the 5 percent cost improvement, the same we had received when we first approached the Indianapolis Water Company about taking over sewer billing. Once again, we chose to test the marketplace.

The prospect of running what would become the two largest privately operated wastewater treatment plants in the United States attracted bidders from all over the world, revealing the large reservoir of private sector talent and experience in the field. Interest in running the plants was so great that the winning proposal came from a company specifically formed to compete for the management of the plants. The White River Environmental Partnership (WREP) was a consortium of the Indianapolis Water Company, the French-owned Suez Lyonnaise des Eaux, and Denver-based JMM Operational Services, Inc. This was a milestone because we had pushed beyond the yellow pages test and discovered that even in areas where a local market did not exist, international companies would come and new ventures would form to respond to opportunities.

Mike Stayton, director of the city's DPW and the lead negotiator for the privatization, said of the WREP partnership: "It's just a different league. These guys have resources our guys could only dream of." WREP brought us some of the best technical experience in the world—the companies comprising the partnership employ more PhD civil engineers than the city of Indianapolis has employees. They literally wrote the book on water treatment.

Through its superior technology and management practices, WREP reduced our operating costs by 44 percent, or $65 million over the five-year contract. WREP saved money by performing preventive maintenance better than its former city counterparts, and its experienced engineers recognized problems more quickly. The company's access to cutting-edge technology helped WREP provide cleaner water at less expense. WREP is currently evaluating a change in the plant's treatment system to ultra-violet disinfection, which kills bacteria better and costs less.

Best of all, WREP's partners possess enormous assets that allow the company to guarantee these savings, ensuring that the city will reduce its costs regardless of whether management can produce the proposed efficiencies at the plants. As of 1997, however, WREP's cost reductions were already substantially ahead of schedule, and the city shared in these gains.

Of course, once again, savings are not the only story. As good as the plants used to be, WREP runs them better. Water quality has substantially improved. Violations of water quality standards, already rare, decreased from about seven annually under city management to one. On average the water that leaves the plants is far cleaner than required by EPA's stringent standards, and is even cleaner than the water it joins in the White River. Councillor Coughenour and the rest of the City-County Council have become believers.

Had we simply accepted that our plants were run better than most government facilities of their kind, and allowed "good enough for government work" to be our standard, we would have lost millions of dollars in savings and substantial technical improvements. By reaching out to a worldwide market of providers, we gained access to the best managers and most advanced technology on earth, yielding cleaner water at almost half the previous price.

Another of our large competitive efforts involved another very well-run government operation: Indianapolis International Airport.

Because of our city's location in the heart of the United States, our airport is an important economic development tool. In 1991, Indianapolis beat fierce competition to land an $800 million United Airlines maintenance facility and the more than 7,000 jobs it will create by the year 2001 (currently 2,500 jobs have been created). Other major arrivals at the airport included a $350 million Federal Express hub, and a $60 million United States postal hub.

Despite these successes, there were reasons to believe that competition might enhance airport operations. As the number of passengers doubled from 1984 to 1994, the airport authority had failed to generate the expected improvements in efficiency that would normally accrue from such growth. Instead, costs per passenger rose 38 percent in that ten-year span. And while the airport industry, as a whole, enjoyed substantial growth in per passenger concession revenue during that time, our revenue had remained virtually constant—representing substantial missed opportunity.

The problem with our airport—the problem with every airport—was that it had no market incentives to operate efficiently. Essentially, an airport operates by calculating its annual budget; subtracting the revenue it receives from parking, concessions, and other services; and charging the difference to the airlines. If expenses go up or revenue goes down—the airport just passes along the additional cost to the airlines, who pass it along to their passengers. There are no consequences for inefficiency.

At first, we considered the outright sale of our airport—an initiative being contemplated in many cities. We rejected this option because of federal regulatory obstacles. Instead, we opted to issue a request for proposals from private companies interested in managing our airport system, putting few constraints on what could be suggested. As a result, the five companies that participated offered a series of brilliant suggestions for redesigning our airport.

One recommended that the airport drop its plan to build a new terminal, redesign the existing terminals, and use the land for commercial development instead. Another pro-

The opportunities for improving service through competition are as boundless as the free market itself.

posed using part of the airport's real estate for a golf course. After a lengthy evaluation process, our airport authority signed a ten-year contract with BAA USA, the American subsidiary of a British company that manages seven airports overseas—handling more than eighty million passengers each year.

BAA projects more than $100 million in savings and increased revenue over the term of the contract, exceeding our most optimistic expectations for private management. The contract guarantees $32 million in savings, and the company is not paid until the first $3.2 million in savings is realized each year.

Under BAA management, landing fees have dropped from $2.49 per passenger in 1994 to $.58 in 1997—a 77 percent reduction. At the same time, net revenue per passenger is up 41 percent, from $2.22 per passenger in 1994 to $3.14 in 1997. We estimate that the airport's cost per passenger, the standard industry measure of efficiency, will drop from $7.78 today to $5.19 by the year 2005, a 26 percent reduction.

These savings are not the product of employee layoffs or salary cuts. In fact, BAA hired all of the existing airport employees, and at comparable wages and benefits. BAA brought down operating costs by drawing on its superior worldwide expertise and bringing the best management practices to our airport. The company increased airport revenue by aggressively courting new retail shops and developing new and better services for airport customers. Instead of viewing an airline traveler as a captive audience for overpriced goods and services—a typical government way of looking at things— BAA negotiates with its tenants to provide an expanded range of retail and what it calls "street pricing." BAA's philosophy is that airline travelers should pay the same price for a pack of gum at the airport that they pay at the corner drug store.

Lower airline fees should have a ripple effect that benefits the airline industry, the city, and the consumer. Airport fees are the fastest rising component of airline operating expenses, accounting for 5 percent of total costs and increasing at twice the rate of inflation since 1988. Our consultants estimate that if every airport in America achieved savings similar to ours, airline operating margins would increase by 30 percent.

Taxpayers will benefit from lower airport costs because Indianapolis's low fees and professional approach will be a magnet for increased economic activity. New maintenance facilities, air-cargo traffic, and airline routes are all rational expectations. Airport passengers may even notice a decrease in airfare as the number of airline routes increases.

Purchasing Outcomes and Solutions

Cheaper can also prove better when private companies can coordinate several services and sell local government what the private sector calls a "total solution." Corrections Corporation of America (CCA) sold us such a solution for a common local headache, jail space.

Like most large cities, Indianapolis suffers from jail over-crowding. The traditional, and complex, public debate is how large a jail to build. The larger the jail, the higher the cost and the more unused capacity. The smaller the jail, the more quickly the facility fills.

When Indianapolis opened up the construction of a new jail for private proposals, CCA submitted a winning idea that completely changed the terms of the public debate. Under the resulting deal, CCA will design, build, and operate a 670-bed facility in Indianapolis. The city will contract to rent 264 beds in the short term, with the option to rent additional beds in future years. CCA will have the right to rent the city's unused capacity to other governments, and will pay the city $3 per day for each bed it rents to someone else. Further, CCA guarantees to pay the city for a minimum of 240 rented beds per day, whether it actually rents them or not.

CCA's proposal will save taxpayers approximately $20 million in construction costs and $1.4 million in annual operating expenses. By selling us an outcome—prisoners housed per day—instead of simply trying to sell us a new jail, CCA opened up new avenues and provided a novel solution to an old and vexing problem.

Creating Profit Centers

Cost savings are not the only financial benefit of outsourcing. Sometimes private companies can raise revenue by increasing the use of discretionary services supported by user fees. The best opportunities often lie in the area of parks and recreation, because government's monopolistic, bureaucratic approach is particularly unsuited to providing amenities. Instead of viewing these services as opportunities, government often treats customers as inconveniences. Increasing the quality of these optional government services can produce big benefits, as our municipal golf courses showed.

Of the many things government does not know much about, running golf courses ranks near the top. Indianapolis has twelve public golf courses, all of which were run directly by city government when we came into office—and all with terrible results. The courses were badly maintained: service was poor; the greens were often brown; and mowing was erratic—some fairways looked like an advertisement for a drunken barber.

The whole experience shouted GOVERNMENT as loudly as the lines at the license branch. Complaints were constant, numerous, and bitter, and those who were complaining were right. The surprising thing was that golfers were still optimistic enough to bother to complain. Hadn't they realized that at government facilities the motto was not "the customer is always right" but "beggars can't be choosers"?

Part of the problem was that with the city in charge, no one was in charge. The golf pros, who were closest to the customers, supposedly oversaw golf operations. But that did not mean much when the greens were mowed by the same parks employees who painted playground equipment, and the golf carts were maintained by the same people who repaired garbage trucks. During one walk-through I asked the pro at the city's premium course how he could let the restrooms slip into such awful condition. His response brought it all home. "The restrooms," he noted sardonically, "are maintained by *your* parks employees."

Now many people—I, for one—do not believe that cities should even be in the golf business. The marketplace will provide inexpensive golf just fine on its own, and if the community decides that allowing poor youths access to golf is a public good, then vouchers would be a much more efficient way of providing it. Instead, the current system essentially taxes poor residents in order to fund subsidized golf for predominantly middle-class, suburban males.

But public golf has passionate constituents, so we concluded that if the city must own golf courses, then at the very least they ought to provide revenue that can be used for core city services.

We opened the management of these courses to competition, allowing golf pros to bid for three-year contracts to manage

> **Competition is like fire. It is an energy source, driving innovation.**

the courses. The city would continue to set greens fees in order to keep the courses accessible, but the pros would have all the authority they needed to run the best courses possible. The pros would maintain the courses with their own supplies and equipment, hire the personnel, operate the snack bar and pro shop, and rent golf carts and equipment. Only by doing all those things well, and at a reasonable price, could the public courses compete for customers. Only by succeeding in that competition could the golf pros prosper.

By this time, the results of competition were no surprise. Within a year golfers noted dramatic improvements. Today, we rarely receive complaints from golfers. Surveys show a high level of customer satisfaction. The number of rounds played increased by 13 percent. Through private contracts, we also increased the number of minority pros managing courses.

Once again, raising quality and cutting costs went hand-in-hand. Out of the business of managing courses, the city identified and sold $330,000 worth of unused golf equipment. Instead of paying the expenses of the golf courses, the city received 20 percent of the courses' revenues—close to a million dollars a year—from the pros, part of which was plowed back into capital improvements for the courses.

There were problems, too. The pros, eager to have improvements ready for the spring golf season, went to work immediately. They

upgraded courses and remodeled club houses. They added or refur-
bished ball washers, yardage signs, flag sticks, tee markers, trash
cans, and golf carts. But laws concerning the expenditure of public
money still applied during the transition to private management,
and the work needed to be publicly bid. The pros, assuming they
had already satisfied public bid requirements when they won the
right to manage the course, blew right by this requirement, and in
the process arguably violated state bid laws.

The incident, covered widely in the local press as a failure of
privatization and used in campaign commercials against me, was
a fascinating collision of old and new approaches to government.
Our golf courses are in fabulous shape. Ninety-four percent of
golfers surveyed say they have noticed improvements. Play is up,
and the city has turned an expense into a revenue source. No one
has ever suggested that the pros were guilty of anything more serious than the sin of enthusiasm to improve the courses, but because
many still measure government by inputs and bureaucratic rule-
following, this competition has been the most criticized of our
administration.

Endless Opportunities

In late 1992, while speaking in New York City about our efforts,
I was asked whether there were any limits on what services could
be moved into the marketplace. Exaggerating to make a point, I
said that city government could be run with a mayor, a police
chief, a planning director, a purchasing agent, and a handful of
contract monitors. My comments found their way into a
national magazine, where they were read by an official of our
city's police union. Not surprisingly, he did not share my enthusiasm for the idea.

The point remains, however, that the opportunities for improving service through competition are as boundless as the free market itself. A final example illustrates the remarkable possibilities that exist when we erase the artificial line between public and private provision of services.

In 1995 the Department of Defense put the city's largest military installation on its list for closure. The Naval Air Warfare Center (NAWC) produced advanced aviation equipment for the Navy, from the Norden bombsights used in World War II to the guidance systems for the Patriot missiles used in the Persian Gulf War. It is the only military facility in the country with the ability to design, model, and manufacture equipment on site.

Losing NAWC would have been a devastating blow to our economy. The base employed more than 2,500 people, and pumped millions of dollars into the local economy. Yet it was philosophically inconsistent for us to complain about federal downsizing when we were committed to the same principle locally. It was unrealistic as well: no community had successfully lobbied the Pentagon to remove a base from the closure list. Our prospects looked bleak. As long as NAWC remained a government military installation, it was not going to stay in Indianapolis. But what would happen, we wondered, if we stopped thinking of NAWC as a government problem with a government solution? We asked the Department of Defense to proceed with its plan to close the facility, but to allow private firms to compete for the right to take over operation of the base. We would spin off NAWC into a private company and sell its services back to the Navy.

After President Bill Clinton endorsed the Indianapolis approach in his letter submitting the closure list to Congress, we had what we needed to move forward. Seven companies submitted bids to assume control of the facility, and in May a selection committee chose Hughes Technical Services Company. Hughes took the risk of managing down costs, finding private sector applications for NAWC technology, and still selling high-quality instruments to the Navy.

The result was an all-around win. The federal government achieved its goal of divesting itself of a military base and avoided a $180 million closing expense in the process. Indianapolis saved more than two thousand jobs, and gained seven hundred more when Hughes decided to expand in Indianapolis. And the former military base is now on the local property tax rolls. All of this occurred because the artificial barrier between public and private was removed.

Chapter Four

Creative Unions

In January 1994 Indianapolis was hit with a particularly nasty blizzard. One of the many benefits of cellular telephones, I discovered, was the increased speed and convenience with which citizens could complain about the city's snowplowing effort. During morning drive time, my phone and those of the morning news programs rang incessantly as motorists enthusiastically expressed their opinions from their cars. These calls shaped the radio and TV commentary, and throughout the day the dissatisfaction grew.

Public works officials provided the usual information on what a great job the city was doing, but complaints seemed unusually high. Snow can ruin political careers, so when the snow eased up the next morning, I visited a city garage where workers were preparing to begin a shift. I asked the drivers—the snowfighters— to gather in one room while I first spoke with the managers in another. I told the fifteen or so managers that I was puzzled by the complaints, and asked their view. One after another volunteered that the plan had been well executed, that everyone was working diligently, and that without vast amounts of new resources, the city was doing the best it could do.

Moments later, I asked the snowplow drivers the same question. Hands shot up. City mechanics should be out on the streets repairing trucks as they broke, reducing down time. Some of their blades were operated by a hydraulic system that broke frequently and needed immediate preventative maintenance. Route maps were hard to read and outdated—they did not reflect current rush-hour traffic patterns, which put some busy streets low on the priority list. To save money, the city no longer used salt with blue dye in it, which had helped snowplow drivers see where they had been and allowed them to notice immediately if their equipment malfunctioned. The new salt came in chunks that often could not go through the spreaders. On and on it went.

These employees did the work, knew the problems, and had workable solutions.

It's funny how few mayors see it that way. On the contrary, many of us view unions as the very embodiment of government inefficiency—that element of city government that keeps costs high and quality low. Everyone knows, after all, that public employees are lazy and incompetent—why else would they work for the government, right?

Wrong. The unions often have little to do with the problem. Public employees are an easy scapegoat, but I invite you to recall the street repair example discussed in Chapter Two. When union workers are given the freedom to put their own ideas into action, they can be as innovative, effective, and cost-conscious as their private sector counterparts—and they can prove it in the marketplace. In fact, since Department of Transportation workers began to compete for street repair contracts, they have beaten the private sector 80 percent of the time. Overall, their costs have dropped, work quality has improved, and the workers have continued to increase their productivity.

"Innovation does not usually happen because someone at the top has a good blueprint. Often, it happens because good ideas bubble up from employees who actually do the work and deal with the customers," writes David Osborne in *Reinventing Government*. The Indianapolis corollary to Osborne's "bubble up" theory is that only competition gives upper management a powerful incentive to listen—because the good idea they hear might be the key to winning the contract.

> **When union workers are given the freedom to put their own ideas into action, they can be as innovative, effective, and cost-conscious as their private sector counterparts—and they can prove it in the marketplace.**

Competitive Unions

We had much the same experience when we decided to tackle the enormous inefficiencies at Indianapolis Fleet Services (IFS), the city agency responsible for managing, maintaining, and repairing the city's fleet of some 2,500 vehicles—everything from snowplows and garbage trucks to road graders and police cars. In 1991, IFS was in bad shape. Costs seemed high, though once again absent competition we had no idea how high. The poor service, however, was beyond question: a backlog of broken graders and patrol cars made five-day waits for repairing a vehicle standard operating procedure. Vehicles and even heavy machinery could be lost in the system for months or even years. Other departments that depended on IFS hated the system—as most captive customers hate any monopoly. The poor service reached such

levels that during my campaign for mayor the Fraternal Order of
Police asked my policy on pay, promotion, crime—and fleet
maintenance.

I told John McCorkhill, the IFS administrator, to outsource
fleet maintenance. John did not disagree, but he did ask me to
delay the bid so that IFS could prepare for the competition and
make its own bid. He knew the agency had a long way to go
before it could dream of competing with the private sector.

Faced with the prospect of competition, IFS streamlined its
operation and upgraded its efficiency and customer service.
Instead of working under foremen, mechanics operated in self-
managed teams. The teams rotated cleanup chores, thereby eliminating outside janitorial services. IFS workers shrank the agency's
inventory and trimmed security costs from 1991 to 1994. IFS
reduced its workforce by 29 percent, from 119 to 84. Over the
same period the agency actually cut its annual budget from $11.1
million to $9.1 million, the lowest amount since 1988.

Once again, we found that most waste came from management,
not workers. IFS's union leader Dominic Mangine alerted us to the
fact that IFS had two managers for every three workers. As
Dominic told us, sounding like a pretty good manager himself,
"Look, I can't carry this overhead and be successful." He was
right, and we eliminated supervisory jobs wholesale to give the
workers a fair chance of becoming competitive. The union bid
reduced the number of salaried employees from forty-two to
twenty.

Perhaps most incredible, IFS workers agreed to forgo the pay
raises previously negotiated by their union (amounting to 10 percent over four years) in exchange for a plan that would pay them
more for generating savings beyond those specified in their proposal. Any additional savings achieved by IFS during the four-year
agreement would be split between the city and IFS employees,

with the city getting 75 percent and the IFS workers 25 percent in the first two years, and splitting 70 percent to 30 percent in the last two years. Pay raises would strictly be tied to performance.

IFS won the contract. The contracted savings from the agreement, coupled with the savings that IFS achieved in the process of making its operation competitive, totaled $8 million over five years.

The union wanted me to fire politically connected Republicans to help a Democratic union look good.

The incentives worked, too. The next year, IFS's operating costs decreased by another 3 percent, despite a nearly 5 percent increase in the number of vehicles serviced. These savings are earning IFS workers some $75,659 in incentive pay, or an average of $800 per worker in the first year.

Interestingly, workers' compensation claims also dropped. In 1988 the average time lost per employee for work-related injuries was 139 hours. In 1994 the average time lost was down to 78 hours, and in 1995 that number plummeted to 22.

Financial incentives are not the only reason injuries, sick time, and absenteeism are down. People come to work because they want to be at work. At IFS morale is up. "I feel like I have some say-so around here now," Dwayne Fletcher, a city mechanic, told the *New York Times*. "Before, nobody wanted to hear your ideas. They were the bosses. We were the workers. There was a lack of respect."

In less than three years IFS made enormous progress, most of it driven by the same union employees who once seemed so hopelessly inefficient. As a result, IFS employees developed such a strong reputation that they now service customers outside of city government—from township governments to social service providers to hospitals. The income produces revenue for the city and increases incentive pay for the workers.

Another outstanding example of how unionized city workers can be just as good as private enterprise employees came from our experience with trash collection. Even before our competition initiative, Indianapolis used private companies to help in trash collection, but no one really knew whether either the private or the public haulers were efficient.

Prior to 1992, the Department of Public Works (DPW) collected garbage through a patchwork system that divided the city into twenty-five districts, which were serviced by DPW's in-house crews and four private haulers. DPW had franchise agreements with the various trash collectors that gave each a monopoly in its service area. Not surprisingly, haulers' prices increased every year. In 1993 the city spent $30 million on solid waste collection.

When the time came to renew contracts in 1993, we opted instead to consolidate the service districts and contract them out. After reducing the number of districts from twenty-five to eleven, we guaranteed DPW one district to ensure that the city retained the capacity to collect trash in case problems arose. We also limited private collectors to a maximum of three districts to prevent a monopoly and predatory pricing.

Once again the administration weeded out middle managers to reduce overhead. Once again union workers reengineered their methods and increased productivity. With the new decision-making freedom, workers decided that all three members of a work crew did not need to ride to the dump when the truck filled up. Instead, a crew could radio in when the truck was nearly full. A lone driver could bring an empty truck to meet them, then drive the full one back to the dump while the work crew went on with its route. It was a simple, brilliant idea that never emerged until competition became a fact.

Winners in the competition ranged from Ray's Trash, a small local hauler, to Browning Ferris Industries, a massive national refuse collection corporation. And the Department of Public Works won three of the ten contracts in open competition, the maximum number possible, actually increasing its market share of the Indianapolis trash hauling business from 40 percent to 52 percent.

Since the new system began on January 1, 1994, the cost per household for trash pickup has dropped from $85 to $68, and DPW crew productivity continues to escalate. The department reduced the number of trash collection crews from twenty-seven to seventeen, while the number of homes serviced per crew increased by 78 percent over the 1992 level. The number of employees declined from 1993 (before competition) to 1995 by about 20 percent. Absenteeism and workers' compensation claims also decreased.

For taxpayers, the competition resulted in a contracted $15 million savings over five years. And once again, city workers, allowed to act like entrepreneurs, outperformed their agreement.

Productive employees beat their own bid price by $2.1 million in 1994. Because of this outstanding performance, in early 1995 we awarded incentive pay to the city workers, averaging $1,750 per worker. The loud applause and cheers greeting me in 1995 as I distributed the checks contrasted sharply with the hissing I received when I met with the same workers on my first day in office in 1992, after a campaign geared to privatization, not competition.

Just as when private companies won, union victories meant better service. Even while reducing prices, the number of customer complaints in union service areas fell 15 percent from the previous year, and the private haulers have even fewer complaints.

When Public Meets Private

Even when private companies win bids, competition can (eventually) improve relations with city workers.

The wastewater treatment privatization discussed previously is a good example of how private businesses can build an important reservoir of goodwill by taking public employee issues seriously. The winning proposal to manage the plants called for the largest employee displacement of any of our competitive efforts. Naturally, our public employee union energetically opposed the deal, packing hearings of the City-County Council and picketing City Hall with signs suggesting that private businesses would pollute the water and endanger public health.

The White River Environmental Partnership (WREP) understood the sensitivity of the situation and decided to recognize the local union, making it one of the few private companies in America to bargain with a public employee union. With WREP's assistance, we placed every single displaced employee who wanted a job. Of the 321 employees working at the plant at the time of the transaction:

- WREP hired 196, twenty more than it needed to run the plant, and relied on attrition to reach its target workforce;

- WREP funded outplacement services that placed forty-three employees in private sector jobs;

- we found immediate jobs for nine employees elsewhere within city government, and placed fifty in a "safety net" where they performed community service work until city jobs opened up; and

- ten employees chose to find employment on their own; eight failed WREP's mandatory drug test or refused to be interviewed; and five retired.

We also discovered that WREP's superior management expertise extended not merely to machinery, but to people as well. Following a bitterly antagonistic relationship between union workers and city managers, employee grievances at the plant were down from thirty-eight in the last year of city operation to an average of one per year under WREP. Employees at the plant are paid wages and benefits equal to or better than their city wages, and they have access to vastly superior training and advancement possibilities.

Two years later, when the city decided to open up the operation and maintenance of the sewer system to competitive contracting, WREP and the local labor union joined to submit a successful proposal.

The Freedom to Compete

Dr. Samuel Johnson is supposed to have said, "The prospect of hanging concentrates the mind wonderfully." It is certainly true that one reason competition works is that it compels workers and managers to question their assumptions—"this is the way we have always done it" is not nearly so strong an argument when you are faced with losing a contract, or even your business, because you are not giving customers what they want.

Nevertheless, a lot more than fear is at work in the competitive marketplace, just as competitors do a lot more than simply respond to consumer demand. Indeed, the crucial factor in a free market is not fear but freedom, the freedom to do your best and use your creative energies to provide better service.

Public employees in Indianapolis were not failing because they were unionized—they were failing because they were monopolized. Not only were they under no pressure to respond to customers, but they were virtually forbidden to do so. At least two forces held them back.

First, the lack of a market prevented public employees from discovering what their customers wanted or even what a reasonable price for their services might be. It may sound good for Republican politicians to denounce inefficient union workers, but how can the average city worker be efficient when not even the top executives in the administration can tell him or her how much it should cost to fill a pothole—or, more importantly, to keep a street in working order? Without market information, no one can know that answer. And a system that does not clearly communicate performance goals to its workers is one that virtually prohibits them from succeeding.

The other force that prevents government workers from serving their customers is the morass of bureaucratic rules in city government that substitute for the demands imposed on private companies by customers. Without market information, government managers must have some grounds for deciding whether a worker is doing enough and have some system for deciding what services will be rendered at what pace and what price. In most cities these rules are a synthesis of imposed regulations (prompted by various concerns from health and safety, to fear of corruption, to civil rights and the environment) and negotiated union contracts. In order to prevent any abuse of discretion, reformers sought over the years to eliminate discretion altogether—that is to say, to eliminate the thought, judgment, and creativity of workers and managers alike—and they succeeded remarkably well. The results govern the workday in great detail, and focus the worker on everything but pleasing the customer.

When market competition refocuses the organization on the consumer, many of these rules—like the rule that required two trucks and eight men on a pothole filling crew—are revealed as arbitrary barriers to the goals of customers, workers, and managers. Competition empowers workers and inspires an entrepreneurial spirit in city government down to the front-line employee level. Focusing on customers—not the rules that substitute for customers—encourages creativity, which increases efficiency and reduces costs. After all, in a free society the definition of value is determined by customer preferences.

Come to think of it, Steve Quick, president of the local chapter of the American Federation of State, County and Municipal Employees (AFSCME), put it much more simply. Because we broke up our government monopoly and allowed city workers to compete to please customers, he said, "city workers are no longer asked to park their brains at the door when coming to work."

Chapter **Five**

Strategic Tools

Shortly after Indianapolis Fleet Services (IFS) employees beat three national firms for the contract to maintain the city's vehicle fleet, an incident happened that turned normal bureaucratic operating procedure on its head. When two employees of the garage quit in the course of normal employee turnover, management did what it always does and posted the vacancies first on internal bulletin boards. The notice quickly disappeared, and after a short time a group of workers submitted a request that the positions not be filled. They offered a plan to pick up the work with the existing staff levels, if a few changes could be made.

This was a truly remarkable proposal, and it came from employees who had participated in Total Quality Management programs for many years. What had changed?

First, obviously, competition. The workers knew they had to stay lean to keep their jobs when contract renewal came along.

Second, IFS employees had access to some new management tools. They had agreed to be measured, and compensated, based on their ability to meet specific performance criteria. With new information at their disposal, the employees knew their costs of doing business, and understood that the salaries of the departing workers went into their bottom line. They also had confidence in their own front-line authority to suggest changes, and the flexibility in their job classifications to carry out their idea.

We came to call this package of management changes our "strategic tools initiative." These tools were essential to our ability to pull the Indianapolis bureaucracy into the competitive marketplace. In a sense, the interesting thing about these tools is how unremarkable they are. The initiatives listed below are simply common sense procedure in the private sector. They became noteworthy only when applied to government's quest to be competitive:

No. 1. Activity-based Costing

Traditional government accounting does not provide the management information we need to reduce costs. Activity-based costing applies private sector accounting techniques to government services with dramatic results.

No. 2. Performance Measures

Simply spending less is not enough. Measuring and rewarding performance are indispensable, requiring us to pay close attention to what we actually produce, and not simply the amount of money we spend on a given service.

No. 3. Popular Budgets

By combining activity-based costing with performance measures, we created a "popular budget" that explained to citizens what they were (or were not) purchasing with every dollar of their taxes.

No. 4. Customer Surveys

Performance must be defined to include customer preferences. Regular customer surveys enable city managers to make informed decisions about tradeoffs in providing various services to citizens, and about awarding incentives as well.

No. 5. Employee Empowerment

As we discussed in the previous chapter, front-line workers often have creative solutions that can greatly enhance operations, but too often bureaucratic rules and unresponsive management prevent them from putting these ideas into action. In order for city employees to succeed in the competitive marketplace, they must be free to carry out their tasks in the manner they see fit. Increasing decision-making authority and freeing workers from narrow job descriptions also allow managers to hold these employees accountable for the results they produce.

ABC

Every year Indianapolis produces one of the best-looking four-color financial reports of any city in the country. But when I took office in January 1992, no one in city government could tell me how much it cost to fill a pothole, pave a street, plant a tree, or pick up trash. Like most governments, Indianapolis did not think in terms of business units or costs. We used standard government accounting principles that prevented our managers from stealing money, but did nothing to stop them from wasting it. We tracked the amount of money spent on salaries, equipment, capital investments, and professional service contracts—but did not break down any of those costs by the individual activities of government.

As a direct result, city employees neither knew nor cared about their costs of doing business.

In the spring of 1992 we hired KPMG Peat Marwick to lead a process called activity-based costing (ABC). For every identifiable activity of government, ABC determines the cost of everything that goes into conducting that activity. The process uses private-sector definitions of depreciation and loads in all the costs of idle equipment, building space, and other fixed costs. In other words, ABC is Accounting 101.

I cannot emphasize enough how utterly elementary such accounting is to running a city. ABC is not a great innovation or a breakthrough in city management. It is merely a mechanism that measures the real costs of providing a service.

Accurate cost information triggered a series of actions by our managers. The first result was the elimination of several egregious examples of waste. When managers in our Department of Public Works analyzed their costs of picking up trash, they discovered $252,000 in repairs over four years on a garbage truck that sold new for $90,000. The city garage employees, with a separate budget, maintained the truck and had no reason to care how many times they fixed the same truck. When we loaded in all costs, we found that taxpayers were paying $39.00 a mile to operate that garbage truck.

We created a reward program, called the "Golden Garbage Awards," to recognize employees who uncovered such examples of waste. Dozens of examples surfaced. A parks employee identified stacks of chalk to line softball fields that had been purchased at year's end by a buyer fearful of having his annual budget reduced if he had any money left over. We had enough surplus chalk to line all the softball fields in the city for five years—even though we had switched to spray-painting the lines two years before.

A manager at our wastewater treatment plant, asked to think about costs for the first time, determined that he could save money by closing down an in-house television production studio that had been constructed so that employees could make their own training videos. When we held a press conference to give him a Golden Garbage Award—a man-bites-dog account of a bureaucrat suggesting his area be reduced—a reporter asked why he had come forward. I cringed, but the unre-

> **Today, the American dream for many is to escape the city for the comforts of the suburbs.**

hearsed response came right from a business school textbook. He simply said that when the city started ABC, and he had to include personnel, equipment, and space in his costs, he realized he could purchase training tapes less expensively than he could make them.

While these examples of eliminating waste were helpful, and made great headlines, the real improvements started when smart managers used the cost information to change the way they worked.

After my post-blizzard visit with the city's snowplowing teams, when I heard dozens of suggestions for improvement from front-line workers, I was eager to see what happened when we applied activity-based costing. We divided the snowplowing groups into regions and then analyzed the costs of each activity associated with plowing snow.

First, we examined all of the equipment used; then all of the materials; then all of the labor for every mile of snow plowed. We discovered the cost of plowing snow varied wildly from region to region. The labor cost of plowing a mile of snow was $39.90 per mile in the central region, but only $13.20 in the southeast region. The cost of materials varied from $48.97 in the southwest region to $9.25 in the northeast region. The total cost for plowing one mile of snow ranged from $117.59 in the southwest region to $39.96 in the southeast.

Now, it may be that differences in topography, road layout, or miscellaneous other factors contributed to some of the difference in cost between regions; but it was clear to us that they could not account for such a huge discrepancy. What we discovered after some pretty elementary investigation actually told us quite a bit.

By examining the numbers, sharing the results with workers, and then applying the best management practice in each region to all the regions, we were able to improve the mix of equipment, resources, and training everywhere. We also unintentionally, but beneficially, started an efficiency competition between the regions. This exercise might seem obvious, yet even now few government organizations possess this basic accounting data. No one cared about numbers when they did not really matter. Managers sought to plow the streets, whatever the cost, whatever the inefficiency.

The most impressive response occurred when a group of public works employees announced in a visit with me that they did not want to pick up litter along city streets anymore. As I began to respond with a predictable lack of enthusiasm, they presented me with a detailed business matrix analyzing their costs.

These workers and their union leadership wanted to redirect their efforts where they could perform the best. They contended that their union wages would never allow them to be competitive in unskilled, low-paying jobs, like picking up trash on the roads. Neither could they compete in areas where the city did not have adequate equipment, such as the machinery necessary to erect temporary fencing at work sites. But given their skills and equipment, the workers concluded they could outperform anyone filling potholes and sealing cracks. They proposed outsourcing litter removal and fencing in order to concentrate on their core business of maintaining streets.

As these examples show, there are benefits to the costing process wholly independent of competition. Indiana AFSCME president Stephan Fantauzzo observed that because of activity-based costing, "We're a better educated workforce now."

Performance Measures

One reason competition works is that it forces managers to focus on the job that needs to be done—the real goal. The very act of bidding out a job makes us ask ourselves not what we have always done but what goal we are trying to accomplish. Once managers begin to focus on the goal and measure performance, the old way of doing things ceases to be sacred and is often revealed to have been absurd.

When the city ran its own tree nurseries (it is hard to forget that we once did something this weird) the goal was, seemingly, to grow trees, which is what the nursery had been doing. But that was not the true goal; it was merely the means to which we had become accustomed. The goal was procuring trees to plant in city parks—or, taking it one more step, the goal was providing attractive public spaces. Seen in this light, and given the thriving private sector market for trees, one has to wonder what on earth could have led city officials to go into the tree nursery business to begin with.

Without clear and specific goals and a way to measure performance, competition would be both impossible and meaningless. Senior Eli Lilly and Company executive and former Reagan administration official Mitch Daniels, chairman of a group of local entrepreneurs that assisted our competition initiative, had a favorite saying: "If you're not keeping score, you're just practicing." That is how we wanted city government to think.

Again, this notion seems elementary. Yet we discovered that no one in city government thought, worked, or managed in terms of measurable outcomes. In a monopoly, with little opportunity for customer pressure and with pay systems based on tenure, no imperative exists to measure performance.

As I walked throughout City Hall, talking with well-intentioned, hard-working employees, virtually nowhere could I find workers or even managers who could clearly state the measured outcomes of their work. Sure, they knew whether a particular task had been completed—a drainage pipe unplugged or a fallen tree removed—but even these basic "outputs" were neither counted, nor monitored, nor rewarded. If these jobs were performed poorly, or not promptly, no remedial action occurred other than the occasional filing of a specific complaint. More complicated and important outcomes such as park, forest, or watershed quality were not even considered.

Even I was guilty. Early in my administration, at a meeting of the city's department directors, I expressed my frustration at our slow progress measuring our performance. I told Mitch Roob, the director of the Department of Transportation, that I wanted to know exactly how many potholes his crews filled in a week. "I thought you wanted to measure performance," he replied. "You shouldn't care how many potholes my department fills. You should care how smooth the roads are. How do you know we're not doing such a poor job filling potholes that we have to go back out and redo them later?" He was right—smooth roads are the goal; filling potholes is only a means to achieve the goal.

We conducted a rigorous effort inside each city department to define performance. Today, every time the city enters into a contract, the agreement stipulates what we expect the contractor to deliver, from smooth streets or mowed medians and parks to major construction projects. We use performance standards internally as well to evaluate and reward city employees and their departments.

Understanding our desired outcomes enabled us to ask more sophisticated questions about whether what we were doing actually helped the people we served. After all, providing unnecessary or unwanted services efficiently should not be a goal of government, nor should cutting the budget of a highly effective and worthwhile agency. Instead, we should direct resources to where they produce the most value for citizens.

An example from my days as a prosecuting attorney illustrates the point. Having determined that making an arrest for domestic violence made the recurrence of violent activity less likely, we devoted considerable resources to more aggressive prosecution of those arrested. Eventually, a researcher asked what should have been an obvious question: does the additional sanction of prosecution over and above the initial arrest further reduce the recurrence of violence?

We implemented a comprehensive approach to city management based on a belief that smaller government is just plain better.

As we soon discovered, the answer in most cases was no. We were devoting substantial resources to doing very effectively something that did not produce the outcome most desired by citizens—a reduction in domestic violence. Clearly that did not mean we should not fully prosecute and seek convictions for those who committed domestic violence. But if our desired outcome was to decrease domestic violence and if we had limited financial resources, then we should have known how to focus our resources to achieve the desired outcome most frequently.

Popular Budgets

Over the years, government budgets at all levels have become enormous, cumbersome documents with mind-numbing layers of funds, subfunds, and technical procedures that render them incomprehensible to the average taxpayer, whose hard-earned dollars pay the bills. It is hard for the people to run their government

or hold their public officials accountable if they cannot understand their government or where their money goes. "Let the buyer
beware" is not a maxim that should apply to government.

Combining our newly determined cost information with our
newly developed performance measures allowed Indianapolis to
create what we called a "popular budget," not so much because
everyone would like it, but because most people would at least be
able to understand it.

A look at the budget that Indianapolis City Clerk John Waters
submitted in 1863 provides an almost humorous example of how
uncomplicated government was back then. The budget totaled a
"whopping" $99,000. A list of expenditures took up twenty-six
lines, and included such items as $8,352 for salaries, $192.73 for
books and stationery, and $50 for a town clock.

Revenue was even more simple. The sources took up twelve
lines on the budget, including $27.33 from a sale of hogs by the
city marshall, and $1.25 from a Mr. Charles Fischer for an "over-
charge on costs." Folks knew where their dollars were going.

The popular budget restores an old dimension to the public
debate about the goals and activities of the Indianapolis city government. Rather than focusing solely on inputs—how much the
city spends—the debate can range freely from broad policy goals
to the cost-effectiveness of individual programs. By spelling out
the precise outcomes that each department hopes to accomplish,
the popular budget invites and facilitates public debate over the
proper goals of city government. And by spelling out the precise
activities that each department performs to achieve its desired outcomes, the popular budget invites debate over whether government activities do in fact achieve their desired outcomes. Most
importantly, the popular budget spells out the cost of each activity performed by the Indianapolis city government and the specific
performance measures by which the activity is judged, putting a

bright spotlight of accountability on everyone in city government, from the front-line workers to the mayor's office itself.

Customer Surveys

In the private marketplace, it is easy to determine what people want: follow their dollars. Do they spend their earnings on vacations? A mortgage? A nice car? Marketplace activity demonstrates what goods and services people value and how much they are willing to pay to obtain them. Because govern-

Without clear and specific goals and a way to measure performance, competition would be both impossible and meaningless.

ment simply confiscates dollars rather than competing for them, government managers do not get good information about their customers' needs and wants. Public officials rarely get feedback from customers in the form of lost business and, moreover, tend to believe their professional training requires them to make decisions for people irrespective of individual preferences. A responsive government must invent processes to determine preferences, including neighborhood forums, focus groups, and public opinion surveys.

A business visit early in my term brought home the importance of basing performance measures on customer preferences. I called on Murvin Enders, manager of the local Chrysler foundry. In his lobby was a sign that said, in essence, "Quality is what the customer wants." Government, on the other hand, often proceeds on the assumption that professional civil servants know how to promote the public good better than taxpayers themselves. So I asked Murvin what happens if his engineers design and build a better engine block, only to have the customers say they still want the one his team views as inferior. He said it quite simply: his company produces value only when it meets customer preferences.

That connected, finally, and we set out to emulate the market by infusing customer input into performance evaluations. Survey data became an important management tool. We used extensive police surveys to measure attitudes about crime among residents of the various Indianapolis Police Department districts. Commanders adjusted their priorities to citizens' preferences. For example, in the south district, where fear of violence ebbed and concern about public nuisances increased, the commander emphasized more enforcement against crack houses and loitering.

Some of the findings were surprising. As part of a complete rebuilding of the city's parks system, we conducted neighborhood focus groups to discuss plans for each park. When asked what services they most preferred in their parks, most people did not answer "playground equipment" or "basketball courts"—they wanted safety. So we shifted resources from less popular programs to create a Park Ranger program to patrol parks and supplement the police presence. The greater sense of safety that resulted increased usage of city parks.

Employee Empowerment

During my twelve years as the prosecutor in Indianapolis, I looked on the municipal requirements of job classifications and job descriptions as a sport. Some bureaucrat associated with city government would tell us the procedures for hiring or transferring an employee, and my administrator's task was to find a way around them. These requirements, however, became more than a nuisance after I became mayor and began downsizing the work force. Our human resources director informed me that I could not transfer a public works employee whose position we had eliminated to the police citizen service desk. The employee was too well qualified, earned too much, and was in the wrong job class, we were told. Because of the employee's good fortune to be in a higher job classification, she was about to lose her job. Lucky her. The war on the central control systems began in earnest at that moment.

Our efforts to dissolve traditional job descriptions had two goals: to push authority down to the front lines and to hold every employee responsible for customer satisfaction. Two examples from our parks department nicely frame the issues.

A year after competing out the management of three swimming pools, I visited a newly restored pool still managed by the city. As I visited the new and beautiful water park in a suburban area, I asked the center manager how many visitors used the facility in the first month and what her net revenues were. She confessed that she had no idea and referred me to the central parks office, which kept track of her revenue and expenses. She had neither the tools nor the authority to manage her center well.

A month later we opened a similar pool in a more urban area, also a city-run facility. I took my two young daughters and set out to be the first visitor. Spotting concrete chips on the ladder up the water slide, I told the girls to jump in the pool while I started sweeping the steps. The project took longer than expected and, as the pool filled with people, I wanted to watch the girls. I asked a young lifeguard to finish sweeping. To this day his answer amazes me: "No," he said, "I'm a lifeguard, not a custodian. Sweeping isn't part of my job." His answer and my response affected his summer (badly) and our approach (well).

When employees have limited control over decisions, it is both unfair and unproductive to hold them accountable for outcomes. And as we repeatedly discovered in our competitive efforts, public employees are more than willing to answer for their results in exchange for real authority over how their jobs are done.

Too many narrowly described jobs reduce effectiveness, increase supervisory costs, and demean workers. When employees are set free, great things happen. One clever group of public works employees, eager to protect themselves against outsourcing, realized that job classifications and supervisors prevented them from responding effectively and quickly to citizens' problems. One group would go to a site and repair a drainage ditch, another group would do spot concrete repairs on the nearby curb, and another might fill the resulting hole in the road.

They grabbed an employee from each area, borrowed an old truck, equipped it with a hodgepodge of tools, and said, "Just let us demonstrate what we can do by ourselves." The team slashed waiting times for priority work from three weeks to two days.

We rigorously eliminated most city job descriptions and classifications, and instituted new data systems that provided center managers with meaningful information upon which to measure performance. These new accounting systems also allowed employees at pools, housing areas, or park centers to purchase necessary parts or equipment immediately, rather than waiting while the centralized purchasing office ordered it.

The Competition Defenses

In just a few years we established a powerful and consistent record of shattering public monopolies and bringing competitive vigor to government. But despite our success we continue to hear many of the same objections over and over again. Five in particular stand out:

No. 1. Competition Reduces Government Control by Turning the Public's Business Over to Private Interests

Because privatization means many things, it is easy for adversaries to threaten the public with "lack of control," presumably suggesting that private vendors will not be responsive to the public. The truth is, we possess many more tools to control the quality and price of a private contractor or winning public employees than we do those employees acting in a typical government bureaucracy. As a result of the bidding procedure, we can impose fines for poor quality or missed deadlines, more easily reward performance, and if necessary simply cancel the contract rather than navigate the excruciating procedures required to actually fire a civil service employee. In each of our competitive initiatives, the city retained and even enhanced its control over services. In all too many American cities, mayors and city managers operating in monopolistic governments have very little control. Competition and marketization dramatically increased government control by giving policymakers more tools for putting their policies into effect and better yardsticks for measuring performance. The only control politicians lose is the ability to hire workers on the basis of patronage instead of productivity.

No. 2. Competition Is Antiworker Because the Lowest-Priced Vendor Will Either be a Nonunion Vendor or be Competitive by Cutting Salaries

This oft-repeated assumption by Democratic opponents of competition is more antiunion than anything we have ever done. Our public employees repeatedly prove themselves to be capable of competing with the private sector and winning, and the idea that they are doomed to failure in the marketplace is insulting. Not only do we let unions fairly and freely compete for contracts, we pay for business consultants to help them prepare their bids. Not a single union worker has yet lost a job due to competition, and salaries have almost never gone down. The self-respect and confidence from competing and winning stands in stark contrast to the usual message to city workers that they are so inefficient or lazy that they must be protected.

No. 3. Competition with Private Firms Is Not Fair

This is true, but not in the way usually understood by critics of competition. Government agencies generally have a running start on their private sector counterparts because they do not have to pay taxes or turn a profit. That translates to about a 25 percent advantage in price. Even with that head start granted government, private firms are all too willing to compete.

No. 4. Privatization Is Patronage

Some argue that privatization is a new form of patronage, replacing traditional city workers with, as one critic wrote, "consultants—lawyers, engineers or other experts brought in on contract—who form Indianapolis's new army of pinstriped patronage workers." Privatization sometimes receives a bad name from sole-source "sweetheart" contracts. The public and the media are rightfully suspicious when a mayor directs a large chunk of government service to a particular firm. We purposely set up a public process, with a special commission, numerous hearings, and testimony about the nominated projects and open competition. Occasionally, a professional service provider would bring us a particularly good idea, winning the right to develop it, but almost always we entertained bids. After all, it is the bidding, not simply the public/private distinction, that produces the value.

No. 5. Private Firms Care for Profits, Not People

Opponents often argue that when competition results in private, for-profit companies providing services, citizens will be hurt. This argument assumes that government employees and government ownership produce public benefits simply because of their government status. In fact, as shown in many of our competitions, the search for satisfied customers produces customer (citizen) value daily. Competition creates incentives to produce more efficient procedures that help better meet the needs of people, and increase customer satisfaction.

Chapter Six

Economic Development and Barriers to Investment

Shortly before I became mayor, a series of calamities rocked the economy of the central city. First, the North American headquarters of RCA-Thomson Consumer Electronics, one of the city's largest and most important employers, left its longtime home on the city's near east side. The company left a neighborhood that was teetering between poverty and prosperity and moved to Carmel, the city's most affluent suburb.

Next, Indiana Insurance Company, a large employer that occupied an entire ten-story downtown office building, decided its building was old and obsolete and moved its headquarters to the suburbs as well.

As these businesses were leaving, plans for a new downtown shopping mall stalled. The city had invested $80 million to buy and prepare land, but no large retail chain would undertake being the necessary second anchor store, and financing for the project was left up in the air. The project left holes in the downtown area the size of entire blocks, putting a blight on the city's image and serving as an apt metaphor for the urban economy.

The severity of the problem hit me during a conversation with Jerry Semler, CEO of American United Life and one of the city's corporate leaders. His company owned the thirty-six–story AUL Tower, one of the landmarks of the Indianapolis skyline. Mr. Semler told me that the annual property tax increases of the 1980s threatened to make the office space in his building—one of the city's most prestigious addresses—noncompetitive.

Once in office, I joined the ranks of mayors trying to bring investment back to urban areas. My three-year effort to bring to downtown the national headquarters of USA Group, a $7 billion guarantor of student loans, provided a case study of the barriers to urban investment.

The CEO of USA Group was a gifted executive named Roy Nicholson, who had built the company from scratch into the nation's largest student loan guarantor. USA Group occupied a beautiful new suburban office park, but the company continued to grow rapidly, and its progressive leadership and civic involvement suggested the company might want to play an important role in revitalizing the city's downtown area. When the city's flagship downtown department store, L.S. Ayres, closed in 1992, vacating a building that took up a full city block, I approached Roy about taking over the building.

Armed with terrific drawings of what the beautiful old building could become, I took my case to Roy, explaining how his headquarters could be the economic and symbolic centerpiece of our plans to save downtown Indianapolis. Roy said that the benefits of locating downtown were worth some additional expense, but the difference had to be reasonable enough to justify the move to his customers, directors, and employees. This seemed reasonable—companies cannot and should not locate in cities out of charity.

At this point, our vision for a new downtown collided with the reality of urban economics. The difference in property tax rates between downtown and USA Group's suburban location was huge. Our proposed renovations triggered a series of federal and state regulations. The old Ayres building would need asbestos remediation to comply with environmental mandates. Major remodeling would be required to bring the building into compliance with federal requirements through the Americans with Disabilities Act. A host of smaller state building codes kicked in. While we had some federal grant money to spend on urban renewal, using it would invoke additional historic preservation requirements. The total cost of government-imposed regulation exceeded $7 million.

With taxes and regulations adding to the cost of bringing USA Group's headquarters and one thousand of its employees into the central city, there was simply no way that locating downtown would not cost a great deal more than remaining in the suburbs.

Roy Nicholson's request articulately, though perhaps unintentionally, summed up the challenge mayors face as they try to halt the flight of wealth to the suburbs. The natural draw of a big city—the diversity, culture, amenities, and architecture—is outweighed today by enormous artificial costs that have been placed on urban economies by bad government policy. High taxes, crumbling infrastructure, stifling regulations, and misguided federal policy all create effective barriers to investment and prevent companies like USA Group from locating in cities.

Across the country, mayors are attempting to address the underlying causes of the flight of wealth by reducing the government-created obstacles to urban investment, with some successes. But

the playing field today is so severely sloped against cities that the
job is arduous and often politically painful.

Taxes and the Flight of Wealth

Driving one day through the section of Indianapolis known as
Castleton, a booming retail center and residential neighborhood
on the city's northeast side, I noticed a startling billboard. The sign
pictured large stacks of money and proclaimed, "Buy a New
Home in Anderson. Save Thousands in Taxes." Anderson is a
growing community located just a few miles north of Indianapolis on Interstate 69; its advertising campaign could have been
repeated by virtually any suburb of a large city in America. The
message is clear. Homeowners and business owners can save thousands of dollars each year by leaving cities and moving to the surrounding counties. Capital is mobile, and people and businesses
will move to places where they can keep more of it.

Mayors of both parties recognize the importance of cutting
taxes. The traditional lines between Republican and Democrat
have blurred at the local level, with remarkable agreement
among a new breed of mayors about the importance of tax-
cutting in reviving urban economies. Consider the following
excerpt from the 1997 budget presentation of Mayor Ed Rendell,
the Democratic mayor of Philadelphia:

> Let me be absolutely clear about this. These tax
> reductions are one of the highest priorities of my sec-
> ond term. If we are to have any chance of permanently
> reversing the decades-long trend of losing residents and
> businesses, we have to continue to implement these
> incremental cuts. We simply cannot, as New York City
> has done, forgo these tax cuts. Improved services are

critical, but they are not enough. Investing in our infrastructure is essential, but it is not enough.... We must
cut the tax burden that chokes our residents, our workers, and our businesses.

Mayor Rendell then continued with the single most important
fact about urban tax increases:

The traditional lines between Republican and Democrat have blurred at the local level, with agreement among a new breed of mayors about the importance of tax-cutting in reviving urban economies.

If we do not, our hopes
of growing our economy
will disappear, and future
mayors and councils will
constantly be arguing
how to divide a shrinking
pie among competing
demands that far exceed
the size of the pie.

Recognizing that higher tax rates produce less tax revenue is
extraordinarily frustrating. The problems of crime and poverty,
the challenge of providing our children with the best possible education, and dozens of other important goals all lead well-
intentioned people to seek more spending by local governments
and schools. Yet the evidence is overpowering. When cities
raise taxes—even to fund vitally important programs—the result
is a faster flight of wealth to the suburbs and more pockets of
poverty.

By implementing the policies described in the first section of
this book, we were able to reverse the trend of higher budgets and
higher taxes. When I took office in 1992, the city budget was
approximately $460 million. By 1997, we cut the budget to $428
million. We did not just cut the rate of growth, or cut the rate of

growth after adjusting for inflation, or use any other accounting gimmick. We actually spent less. For the purpose of comparison, if the budget had continued to grow at the rate it did through the 1980s, the 1997 budget would have topped $547 million, about 36 percent higher than our actual budget.

Following fifteen property and income tax increases in the 1980s, the shrinking budget allowed us to halt the progression of higher taxes and reduce taxes twice in five years, with a third cut pending.

Despite our success reducing the size of government, Indianapolis city government is still the tail wagging the dog. In 1997 the total property tax rate for a home owner in downtown Indianapolis was $12.55 per hundred dollars of assessed value. Of that, only $3.80 went to the city of Indianapolis. The rest went to dozens of government agencies inside the city with the authority to raise taxes, with schools taking up a whopping $5.58. From 1992 to 1997, while the city was reducing its tax rate, taxes to support township government increased 35 percent, and school taxes exploded, increasing by 40 percent.

I watched in frustration as taxes continued to rise through the actions of little-known, often unelected boards. School boards wanted more buildings, more teachers, and more technology. Metro wanted more buses. Libraries wanted more books and better buildings. Everybody wanted better salaries. Even in smaller, Republican enclaves where candidates had run against higher taxes, raising taxes often turned out to be easier than making tough management decisions.

With virtually no legal authority to wield, I resorted to the bully pulpit. I invited every member of every governing body with the authority to raise taxes to a summit. The invitation list included more than two hundred names. I reasoned, argued, and pleaded with them to join in a commitment to lower taxes. The response from the seventy or so who chose to attend ranged from polite silence to outright hostility.

The conversations I had with school board members and other officials made it clear that most officials whose responsibility did not include economic development, by definition, wanted to raise taxes. Ironically, these same officials complained about the city's use of tax abatements to stimulate economic development. When I agreed to curtail the use of tax abatements if they would freeze their tax rates, the conversations ended quickly.

All the municipal corporations—transit, library, and hospital— face enormous demands for services. Like schools, these entities evoke a certain sympathy for higher taxes, and the City-County Council routinely approved tax hikes on their behalf. Not to do so would be perceived as being stingy with services that are essential for the public.

One of the most difficult fights was with the library board, which wanted $58 million for a building program. The library board was quite adept at using the Washington Monument gambit. It had recently completed construction of a multimillion dollar administration building, but when I opposed their tax increase I was accused of being against books for children in poor neighborhoods. A fascinating side debate occurred over the library's policy of using tax dollars to purchase entertainment movies. Should libraries be in the business of providing taxpayer-funded copies of "Die Hard" and other movies? I would argue no. Each tax increase makes the city less competitive, makes it harder to attract businesses, and creates less, not more, tax revenue. This scenario repeats itself in city after city.

Hoping to stop the bleeding, public officials began to compensate for their high taxes by offering tax breaks and financial incentives to lure companies downtown. As competition grew stiffer among cities and, more notably, between cities and their suburbs, the incentive packages got larger and larger.

As the barriers to investment worsened, the incentives increased. Indianapolis was guilty as well. In 1991, about one week before my election as mayor, Indianapolis and Indiana assembled a financial package that lured United Airlines to develop a massive maintenance facility at Indianapolis International Airport. United Airlines will eventually invest at least $750 million dollars and employ six thousand people in Indianapolis as a result of the deal, causing some national observers to call it the economic development jewel of the year. United Airlines, a great corporate citizen, is keeping all of its promises of investment and job creation, and is helping establish the airport as the preeminent aircraft maintenance center in the country. But Indianapolis taxpayers will be paying for the deal until the year 2017.

Tax incentives and financial assistance are easy. Elected officials get to cut ribbons and take credit for creating jobs. Using tax dollars to compensate for high taxes, crumbling infrastructure, or overly burdensome regulations is easier than actually addressing the problems themselves. When used in this manner, abatements are truly unsustainable development—a finger-in-the-dike solution to serious structural barriers to urban investment.

The new mayors are sandwiched in between the desire to end the practice of financial incentives, and the recognition that they remain a necessary tool. In the end, bringing the USA Group downtown required us to use proceeds from a tax increment financing district to help reduce the costs. This type of financing allows city officials to borrow money for infrastructure and pay it back from the future additional taxes that the business will pay on the new investment. We used these funds to remove asbestos and resolve other code problems with the building before we transferred it to the USA Group.

Many cities, like Indianapolis, have compromised by adopting specific standards for the use of financial incentives, and have required companies to pay back their incentives if they failed to meet their written commitments for investment and job creation. When deciding whether to provide assistance, Indianapolis considers how many jobs will be created, how many jobs will be retained, the wage levels of the new jobs, the amount of the company's capital

Regulation kills the urban economy with a thousand pinpricks.

investment, and the impact of the new investment on the surrounding neighborhood. No assistance is given to companies offering low-paying jobs or no capital investment, and greater assistance is provided to companies that offer higher wage levels and commit to hiring from areas with higher unemployment. Using these stricter policies, Indianapolis has reduced the total amount of abated assessed value by 18 percent.

Suburban Competition

As the Anderson advertising campaign showed us, outlying cities often employ aggressive tactics to lure businesses away from the center city. They often do this simply for growth's sake, without really examining the benefit to their taxpayers. Some economic development officials in these areas measure their success by body counts alone—i.e., the gross increase in new jobs—while ignoring the long-term effects of their actions. Ironically, there is often more political benefit in one job "created by government economic development programs" than ten created indirectly by small government.

One example from Indianapolis involves two wealthier suburbs that adopted curious policies for manufacturing and office expansion. The cities of Lebanon and Plainfield, both in counties adjoining Indianapolis, provided infrastructure subsidies and ten-year abatements to attract existing Indianapolis companies. Even though their cities had very low unemployment, they taxed their residents to offer incentives to new employers. Because of the low unemployment, some existing employers in the area (whose taxes helped pay for the incentives) lost workers to the new businesses.

A popular response for many cities is annexation, which occasionally makes a great deal of sense. In Indianapolis, then-mayor Richard G. Lugar helped set Indianapolis on its present successful course when he merged city and county government in 1970 to create a system called Unigov. However, today there appears to be a movement toward annexation without a careful look at whether the resulting government is better. Instead, it has become an easy way out for urban areas that have lost their tax base. They are essentially giving up entirely on the prospect of attracting jobs. They are saying that their economies have become so noncompetitive that they cannot produce more taxes through economic growth, so they have to seize it through annexation.

But annexation without addressing the fundamental problems will only force people further into the suburbs.

Rather than battle our suburbs in an economic development war that hurts both, we decided to try negotiating a peace treaty. We assembled a group of elected officials from the surrounding counties to address regional issues and promote awareness among our suburbs that their future is linked to the city core. Regional business leaders formed the Metropolitan Association of Greater Indianapolis Communities to further the cooperative agenda. We repeatedly emphasized that the downtown area served the heart of the region psychologically, symbolically, and financially. City development officials distributed to elected officials and reporters a study by the National League of Cities, which showed that although urban losses sometimes create short-term suburban gain, they almost invariably hurt suburbs in the long term.

Thinking through the issues, we hoped, would persuade the officials to rechannel their naturally parochial instincts. After two years we reached a "bilateral treaty" with the most prosperous adjoining county. This agreement provided, among other things:

- shared infrastructure investment,
- regional transportation and sewer planning,
- shared strategies for targeting key industries, and
- no economic cannibalization.

Cities must resolve their own structural problems. Simply enlarging the circle of wealth redistribution through annexation does not do that. Yet at the same time, suburban businesses and residents must understand the need for the regional economy to expand together, and that today's edge city will be threatened tomorrow if the concentric circle of poverty and despair continues to grow.

Infrastructure

No description of the government-created barriers to investment in cities would be complete without a word on the crumbling of America's urban infrastructure.

The day after I took office, the Indianapolis Chamber of Commerce presented me with the Getting Indianapolis Fit for Tomorrow report, which identified more than $1 billion in overdue repairs to the city's infrastructure. The city had accumulated a massive hidden deficit in deteriorating streets, sewers, bridges, and parks. And Indianapolis is in relatively good shape for a major city—most older cities have even greater infrastructure needs.

Deferring repairs any longer could lead to insurmountable costs in the future. But the report proposed funding the infrastructure improvements by increasing sewer user fees by $111 million over ten years, raising stormwater discharge fees by $283 million over ten years, issuing bonds of $204 million from property taxes, and creating an "infrastructure income tax" to raise $478 million over ten years.

Here is where our efficiency efforts really paid off. We knew raising taxes was not an option. The Indianapolis competition effort was designed not just to save money, or even just to produce city services more effectively. It was a way to free up operating dollars to reinvest in critical infrastructure problems. Not only did we refinance existing city debt, but we also borrowed against the real, established annual savings from competition. Without raising taxes we created the largest capital investment program in the history of Indianapolis.

As if to emphasize the importance of rebuilding our infrastructure, just weeks before we announced the Building Better Neighborhoods program, two sewers collapsed in downtown Indianapolis.

Businesses expand only where a city's services can support them. Good transportation and functioning sewers literally produce the foundation for growth.

Regulation

Regulation kills the urban economy with a thousand pinpricks. Excessive regulation increases the cost of doing business, which drives existing businesses out of cities and discourages others from moving in. State and local officials like to point the finger at the federal government, which does bear an enormous portion of the blame. Still, many local governments can hardly complain, given the regulatory problems they impose on themselves.

To put in context the accumulated regulatory sludge that clogs the economic engines of cities, consider this. Indianapolis, by all standards, is historically a small government city. Yet I inherited a regulatory code that was 2,800 pages long and had never been subjected to scrutiny. Some regulations were comical, like regulating the sale to minors of "sneezing powder, itch powder or stink bombs," or requiring licenses for shooting pigeons and milking cows within the city limits. Most were serious, hurting business growth and often failing to produce the intended good. I cannot imagine some of the market-killing regulations of cities with traditions of big government.

Mayors want a marketplace that works and produces wealth because it is free of misguided government interference.

How do these regulations make it on the books? A great example occurred when several local fire department officials visited me to lobby for a municipal fire code much more rigorous than state regulations. After a two-hour presentation it struck me that no one in the room had said one word about how the costs of their proposals compared to their benefits. At first I found this extraordinary, but as I thought about it, it became obvious. The fire chiefs had a responsibility to prevent fires. Period. If the lower rents of an older building could not support the price of a full sprinkler system, it simply was not their problem. There was nothing to balance their professional commitment to their job.

So we created a balance. We established the Regulatory Study Commission (RSC) to act as a counterweight to the good intentions of bureaucrats and other well-meaning regulators by examining existing regulations and helping to eliminate outdated, unneeded, and often counterproductive rules. We obviously did not want to eliminate regulations that really did protect public safety and health. But we did want to adopt the philosophy that government interference is a last resort for solving problems. We wanted to ensure that the costs of any given regulation did not exceed the benefits it created for the community. We also felt that local regulations should not exceed state or federal standards without an overwhelming and compelling local reason.

One of the RSC's most important battles involved asbestos regulations that were adopted by a local board and headed to the City-County Council for passage. If approved, it would have been one of the most stringent asbestos abatement regulations in the country—far exceeding Environmental Protection Agency standards. The RSC concluded that the proposed stringent regulations would not improve worker safety or enhance environmental protection, but would cost residents and businesses $8 million to $20 million a year—not including jobs lost through the creation of yet another economic incentive for businesses to decide against relocating or expanding in Indianapolis.

We were able to convince the City-County Council to reject the proposals, yet to this day we continue to fight equally ineffective, if not harmful, regulatory strategies.

Another regulatory barrier comes from government rules specifying in unyielding detail the procedures businesses must follow to achieve a government-specified good. Too often, what gets lost in the process is whether the desired outcome is being achieved.

For years the Meridian-Kessler neighborhood endured a vacant gas station on a prominent retail corner. Before a prospective buyer could build on the property, some cleanup of the site would be necessary due to the former presence of underground gas tanks.

This in itself would not have been too large a hurdle for potential investors to manage. The state's Department of Environmental Management, however, advised that it would require any buyer to perform cleanup well beyond the boundaries of the property. Following state rules, a buyer would have to drill in the adjoining road and in the yards of homes neighboring the property. The buyer would be required by law to clean up any oil and gas contamination it found—even though the road was paved with oil-based asphalt and an active station with its own problematic underground tank was right across the street.

Not surprisingly, investors repeatedly walked away from these restrictions. Thus, because state regulators insisted on a costly and bureaucratic process, the site remained vacant for years. Rather than welcoming the prospect of cleaning up the site, inflexible state regulators ensured that the property remained vacant and contaminated. Through repeated meetings with state regulators, environmental experts, and a prospective buyer, we were able to show that the buyer's cleanup plan would satisfy health and safety concerns. However, we only succeeded in getting an exception, not in changing the system. For the next cleanup, the process will start all over.

The Federal Obstacle

Federal urban policy drives wealth out of cities. In fact, if we specifically designed a "suburban policy" to drive investment out of cities, it would look a lot like the current system.

First, the federal government devoted the lion's share of our federal transportation dollars to subsidizing the construction of interstate highways. John Norquist, the Democratic mayor of Milwaukee, is particularly eloquent on this issue:

Nothing could be better calculated to destroy cities than America's current transportation policy.

The basic value of a city is the proximity of its people to its markets, which create wealth and culture. Since 1956, the federal government has spent hundreds of billions of dollars to gouge our urban centers with six- and eight-lane freeways, which separated people and markets. The freeways dispersed the economy, destroyed thousands of homes and businesses, and sucked millions of middle-class residents and businesses out to the suburbs.

City residents, of course, paid for our own degradation. Almost every new suburban home came with a big mortgage, the cost of which was artificially lowered in most cases by a cheap FHA loan, a hefty mortgage deduction, or both.

The second strategy of the federal antiurban policy was to pass a series of regulations that are politically popular but have a disproportionate impact on urban areas. Components of this strategy include environmental cleanup requirements, the Clean Air and Clean Water acts, application of the Davis-Bacon Act, and the Americans with Disabilities Act, to name just a few. All of these are federal versions of the sprinkler ordinance proposed by our fire department. Each has a laudable goal, but each was passed without any regard to its impact on the local economy.

Rigid environmental regulations virtually quarantine dozens of urban sites, known as brownfields, from development. Just south of downtown Indianapolis is an abandoned industrial site with easy access to interstate highways and rail lines. Yet it remains undeveloped, not so much because of the cleanup cost, but because of the fear of environmental liability. It is much cheaper and easier for businesses to chop down some trees and develop a site in our suburbs.

The Clean Air and Clean Water acts add billions to local budgets, forcing cities either to raise taxes or divert dollars from infrastructure or other pressing needs. Cities will disproportionately bear the burden of the $60 billion cost of new EPA air quality standards.

> Disregard for the Tenth Amendment has ominous consequences: it endangers the very construct upon which the whole American experiment is based.

The Americans with Disabilities Act is particularly difficult. No one could argue with the goal, yet Mayor Rendell estimates that simply bringing Philadelphia's curbs and sidewalks in compliance with the ADA will cost Philadelphia $140 million—more than three times his annual budget for street repair. Why? The ADA contains some of the most minutely detailed specifications ever issued by Congress. Under this statute, cities like Indianapolis negotiate with the Justice Department the precise angle of slope on sidewalk ramps they want to construct.

The Davis-Bacon Act, as it is currently enforced, is one of the lesser-known barriers to urban investment. Eager to develop deteriorated retail corners in urban areas, we used federal Community Development Block Grant money to employ urban youths in construction, painting, and fixup. We were to provide a much-needed fixup while teaching job skills to young people. The enforcers found us again: Davis-Bacon rules require cities to pay the prevailing wage on projects funded with federal dollars. So much for that project. Thanks to the federal government's help, we had to choose between completing the project with skilled labor and giving up on our idea of using the opportunity to train youths, or forgo the federal dollars and train the youths knowing that we would not have the funds to complete the renovations.

The third strategy of the federal antiurban policy was to create a poverty industry that totally overrides the operation of the marketplace. Through Aid to Families with Dependent Children, the federal government pays young teenage mothers cash benefits only if they do not work and do not live with their families. The federal government creates a marginal tax rate of nearly 100 percent on the working poor, discouraging people from entering the workforce. The federal government requires local governments to build and operate huge public housing complexes, making government the biggest slumlord in virtually every major city, instead of simply allowing the poor to make housing choices in the marketplace.

Mayors do not want more programs, or bigger federal checks. They want a marketplace that works and produces wealth because it is free of misguided government interference. The federal government could help by choosing local control, the free market, and individual choice over federal bureaucracies.

Use Regulatory Relief to Encourage Investment in Cities

Washington should stimulate urban economies by modifying dozens of mandates that have a disproportionate effect on older urban areas. For example, a more flexible approach to environmental regulations would not only remove a barrier to investment, but also allow cities to do a better job cleaning up brownfields, each of which has a unique set of needs based on the nature of the contamination and the proposed use for the site.

Replace Federal Grants with Tax Cuts

Washington should pursue real empowerment by eliminating "good deed" urban programs in favor of broad block grants or tax cuts for residents of cities. If the federal government really wanted to help, it would scrap the subsidies and replace them with a tax break for residents of cities, really letting the marketplace work. Markets, not mandates, are what cities need from the federal government. Interesting, again, is the fact that Republicans and Democrats at the local level are agreed upon the barrier that the federal government places on urban investment. The *New Democrat* editorialized:

> Here's a suggestion. Empowerment zone enthusiasts defend their idea as an experiment. Fair enough. But at the same time we test whether empowerment zones can revive dying districts, let's conduct another experiment. For two years, let's allow a major city to forgo all federal aid in return for which it and its citizens will be relieved from federal regulations and taxes. Would such a city be better or worse off? It's worth finding out.

I know a dozen mayors who would jump at the opportunity to try such an experiment.

Reducing the tax differential, rebuilding infrastructure, cutting regulations, and fighting the federal regulators can pay off, and using financial incentives sparingly and prudently can pay off. Over the past five years Indianapolis has taken off with record job growth and investment. The city's population, relatively stagnant for fifteen years, is growing today. During this period, the city experienced four consecutive years of record home construction and job creation. The current unemployment level is the lowest since the city began keeping records.

In September 1995 Circle Centre Mall opened to great fanfare. The holes that marred the downtown area are gone, the shopping center is beating all predictions for sales, and new restaurants are popping up all around. Less than five years after L.S. Ayres closed its doors, retail is alive again in downtown Indianapolis.

In April 1997 the first of one thousand employees of USA Group moved into the newly restored Ayres building in the heart of downtown. The vitality and excitement associated with the move and the psychological lift seemed well worth the slight deviation from our preference to allow the market to work its magic without us.

Nevertheless, no amount of tax abatements will be able to bribe businesses and restore a city to economic health. Long-term success depends more on continuing to eliminate government-created disincentives. Once the playing field is leveled cities will again naturally grow and produce opportunity.

Chapter Seven

An End to Social Programs

For three decades, cities suffered the consequences of misguided welfare policies. Urban economies were nearly destroyed as the middle class headed for the suburbs and welfare subsidized the poor to remain outside the mainstream economy. Welfare made work not merely unnecessary, but irrational for many well-meaning single mothers trying to care for their children. By making no distinctions between those who want to work but need help, and those who simply choose not to work, welfare eroded the work ethic. Welfare also removed the consequences for teenage pregnancy and fatherhood, condemning many children to poverty from birth.

One of the hopeful signs for the future of cities is the consensus that now exists that welfare failed—not merely because it cost too much, but because it failed to help people in need get back on their feet. The federal government finally ended the lifelong welfare entitlement, and is slowly passing authority for public assistance to the states. Creative approaches are springing up across the country, many with promising early results. As important as these changes are, they only set the stage for the work that must take place.

Getting people off welfare is easy. Shorten the time limits for receiving benefits, and tighten the eligibility requirements. Several states, including Indiana, have already begun this popular but superficial strategy. Caseloads will drop, but not for the right reason. More residents of inner cities will join the growing segment of society that is unemployed and not looking for work.

The hard task—and the critical challenge for cities—is to bring people back into the workforce. Welfare as a social program must cease to exist. In its place should be transitional help, job placement, and family rebuilding. Each program should be flexible enough to meet the individual needs of its customers, measured on results, and paid for performance. Public assistance will be the bottom rung of a ladder toward self-sufficiency.

First, the authority leaving Washington must pass through the state governments and continue down to the local level. Replacing bloated, unresponsive federal bureaucracies with bloated, unresponsive state bureaucracies will not do much to help the poor. Bringing the poor back into the mainstream economy is a painstaking task, done one person at a time. Strategies must be designed at the local level to be effective.

Second, the welfare delivery system must be dismantled and replaced with a flexible system that reflects the enormous complexity of reasons why people are poor and unemployed in America. The best way to create such a system is through the marketplace—with performance-based, competitively awarded contracts.

Welfare Pays More than Work

For twelve years as prosecutor, like many district attorneys, I was responsible for collecting child support from "deadbeat" fathers. Every AFDC mother in the city was my client, and I got to know many of them pretty well. They were not the stereotype of welfare recipients. They understood quite well how the system worked, and knew that if they entered the work force they would lose health care, pay more for their public housing, and incur transportation and child care costs.

In other words, *the welfare system did not make work unnecessary—it made work irrational*. What kind of mother, at any income level, would take a job if it meant her children

All able-bodied members of society, for their own benefit and for the benefit of their community, should be productive participants in the economy.

would be worse off? As Robert Woodson, president of the National Center for Neighborhood Enterprise, notes, "The first thing we must do is understand that poverty may make a person dispirited and frustrated but it does not make a person stupid."

Many welfare clients are resourceful, practiced customers of social services. Like customers, the poor assess welfare "products" based on how they fit their own lives and goals. In a startling article in the Manhattan Institute's *City Journal*, Arthur Schiff wrote about Rose Johnson (the name had been changed), a woman on welfare in New York City who took four separate training courses for a career as a word processor. Rose, who had young children, did not want a job. She had no intention of even looking for work, but enrolling in job training programs allowed her to receive certain stipends. As a veteran of training programs, Rose knew which paid for transportation, lunch, child care, and even clothes. She knew how to work the system. In one program she convinced the welfare department to allow her assistance for two bus rides to training, then walked one bus line every day and pocketed the difference. Schiff writes:

> For those truly interested in the welfare of the poor, this is good news, because it suggests that the poor are inclined to run their own lives and are mostly capable of doing so. The bad news is that social service programs elaborately designed to make the poor behave in certain ways, don't. They simply become part of a stream of family income, a package poor people put together to live on.

Rose Johnson behaved in a completely rational manner. The system itself was irrational. For more evidence, consider the case of a woman in Indianapolis who applied for transitional benefits (benefits that are offered to welfare recipients during their transition to employment) that would enable her to accept a job she had secured in the private sector. Consulting a welfare caseworker, she found that eligibility for transitional benefits is restricted to those who have been on AFDC for at least three months. The system's solution to this dilemma? Enroll the mother in AFDC for three months. Not surprisingly, her prospective employer could not wait and gave the job to someone else.

In 1993 an Indiana University professor estimated that the benefits package of welfare in Indiana equaled $7.50 an hour, at a time when our beginning wage averaged $6.50. In 1995 the Cato Institute released a fifty-state study estimating the value of Indiana's package even higher, at $9.20 an hour.

Every day I talk to business people in Indianapolis who echo the problem. My first run-in occurred early in my term when I took some clothes to a neighborhood tailor for alterations. I asked the owner, a European immigrant, about his business. He said that business was so good that the long hours were killing him. When I asked why he did not hire some help, he pointed to a "help wanted" sign in the window offering $8.00 an hour for seamstresses—reasonable wages by Indianapolis standards. No one wanted to work for him, he informed me, unless he paid them off the books, in cash. The applicants would lose more in welfare payments than they would make working for him.

I had a similar experience the next year while I was meeting with several owners of central Indiana McDonald's franchises. While I talked about the city's robust economy and low unemployment rate, they complained about the growing difficulty of attracting workers. Many were offering starting salaries of up to $7.50 an hour, health benefits, and even signing bonuses. When I asked with whom they competed for labor, their answer surprised me. They replied that the welfare department was their chief competitor.

Eroding "Marketable Character"

While some recipients of public assistance are smart consumers of government products, others simply no longer have a work ethic. Again, the welfare state is at least partially culpable: it sends the message that work is optional.

Take for instance the very large, tough young man I confronted during a hot summer night when tempers were flaring between the police department and several disruptive youths. Attempting to mediate the confrontation, I spoke with a small group of the protesters. After we exchanged views, his about the police, and mine about the limits of acceptable protest, the man complained about a lack of jobs in the city. I told him there were thousands of jobs available immediately and offered to help him start work the next day, but he declined—no McDonald's job for him! I then offered to find him a job paying $35,000 or more as a truck driver—just the week before, industry leaders complained to me that they needed more than eight hundred additional drivers. This time, the young man did not like the hours.

Dennis West, president of Eastside Community Investments, one of the nation's preeminent community development corporations, calls the missing ingredient "marketable character." West points out that those of us who participate in the mainstream economy must possess certain attributes (albeit to varying degrees) in order to maintain employment, including, among others, understanding the importance of showing up to work, on time, every day; showing respect for superiors; and being polite to customers. People who possess these basic skills can secure virtually any entry level job in today's economy. These attributes are of no use to individuals trapped within the welfare system, and thus people who have spent many years in the system do not develop marketable character.

Welfare Subsidizes Bad Behavior

The basic welfare program we now know as Aid to Families with Dependent Children (AFDC) was originally created as part of the Social Security Act, one of the cornerstones of Franklin Roosevelt's *New Deal*. Then called Aid to Dependent Children (ADC), the purpose of the program was to provide financial support for children who were "deprived of parental support or care," almost always because of the death of the family's principal breadwinner. In 1935, 85 percent of children received ADC because of a father's death.

By the 1960s that had changed—some 93 percent of families were on the program (renamed AFDC in 1950) because a father had left home or never lived there in the first place. Divorce or desertion had replaced death as the most common reason for the absence of the father from the home. A program that began in one era with the best of intentions—providing help for families who had lost their primary source of income through no fault of their own—had, in a different era, become a subsidy that encourages families to break up and fathers to ignore their responsibilities to their wives and children.

One of the hopeful signs for the future of cities is the existing consensus that welfare has failed.

Author Charles Murray observes:

> [T]hough the country truly does spend a lot of money on welfare, it is not obvious that money is really the problem. Suppose that for $210 billion we were buying peaceful neighborhoods and happy, healthy children in our low-income neighborhoods. Who would say that the nation could not afford it?
>
> Instead…the main source of the nationwide desire to do something about welfare is grounded in the concerns about what welfare is doing to the health of society. Judging from all that can be found in the press, on talk shows, and in the technical literature, an unusually broad consensus embracing just about everyone except the hard-core Left now accepts that something has gone drastically wrong with the family, that the breakdown is disproportionately found in poor neighborhoods, and that the welfare system is deeply implicated.

For twenty years state and federal governments prohibited an intact family from staying together if either spouse sought to collect welfare. By conditioning payment on the absence of a father, welfare subsidized teenage parenting. Until last year a young woman in Indiana could receive assistance only if she did not live with her mother. In other words, if she wanted a child and her own home, she could have both at public expense.

We have been purchasing bad behavior and aggravating one of the most disastrous trends in modern society. The welfare system breaks what should be the cardinal rule of government: do no harm. Government taxed citizens and then subsidized the destruction of the family and of the work ethic—using tax dollars to undermine core values of most of those very taxpayers.

Break Up the Welfare Monopoly

Mayors and local officials are trying to change the rules and incentives of welfare. Common reforms include requiring work of some form in return for any benefits; insisting that teen mothers live at home and attend school; increasing child support enforcement; and providing incentives for fathers' involvement.

Yet all of these reforms will fail unless accompanied by a complete overhaul of the welfare delivery system. The current system was created to administer a massive, one-size-fits-all federal program that delivered checks to the poor efficiently and with the fewest mistakes. The resulting regulation-bound bureaucracy, which measures itself on the number of processing errors instead of the number of customers returned to the work force, was designed to keep people in the system.

By its design, the existing welfare bureaucracy is incapable of doing anything else. Caseworkers do not have the authority, resources, or incentives to provide the tailored responses necessary to get their customers back in the work force. Welfare officers are not allowed to make distinctions between those who want to work but need help, and those who simply choose not to work. The bureaucracy is particularly unsuited to perhaps the most important job of all—rebuilding families.

To understand why the existing welfare bureaucracy is incapable of implementing these reforms, follow a typical welfare recipient in Indianapolis before we implemented our pay-for-performance system:

A single mother applies for AFDC at the welfare office. She is assigned a case number and

Welfare as a social program must cease to exist. In its place would be transitional help, job placement, and family rebuilding.

asked a series of questions that determine what benefits she is qualified to receive. She is then referred to the state employment office for help in finding a job. The employment office assigns the new welfare recipient another case number, and asks about her job skills and work experience. Her background is matched against job openings listed in the employment office's computerized database, and if no immediate matches are found, the woman is sent on her way with instructions to return within a specified period of time.

And so it goes. The woman, if she actually does want to get a job, returns to the employment office faithfully. If nothing obvious is available, her visit is dutifully logged in, and off she goes again. When a match does occur, she may receive a notice in the mail a few days later telling her to show up at a certain place at a certain time for an interview. Transportation to the interview and child care are up to her.

A former welfare recipient in Indianapolis says that the welfare office usually provided no details about the job opening, no coaching for the interview, or any other help. "I would have no idea what the job was, or who I was supposed to talk to, or how

I was supposed to find transportation there." Often, the job was filled by the time the interview rolled around. Another former welfare recipient, testifying at a hearing of the Indianapolis welfare planning council, told of making $5.50 an hour participating in a local welfare-to-work program, but desperate to earn more. When asked if her caseworker had done anything to help her find a better-paying job, the answer was a simple no.

What is so tragic—and sadly typical of welfare and employment offices in most cities—is not merely that the system fails to connect people with jobs. What is tragic is that everyone behaves exactly as they are supposed to. No one is accountable for helping welfare recipients get a job. I spent an afternoon with intake officers in the state-run county welfare department trying to learn more about this warped system. The caseworkers I spoke with were well intentioned but their comments were revealing. They stressed that their job was to determine eligibility with the fewest errors. That focus makes all the difference, and it explains how someone like our typical welfare recipient could become lost in the system.

What are the consequences for the welfare office when welfare recipients do not find jobs? There aren't any. By reimbursing almost all administrative costs without imposing any meaningful performance measurements, the federal government offers local offices a bargain. The more they spend, the more they get. Results do not matter.

Most proposals for reform include the important step of reducing or ending assistance for those who refuse to work. Yet our typical welfare recipient is an all-too-real example of why this will fail unless the existing welfare delivery system is scrapped. The new system will prove even more cruel to the poor than the old system by trapping welfare recipients in a broken system for two years, then kicking them out.

Competitive, Performance-Based Contracts

Breaking up the welfare bureaucracy would give smart consumers of social services, like Rose Johnson, the ability to redesign the welfare system through their choices. Allowing many vendors to compete for clients will force social service providers to be customer-oriented and promote innovation. By exercising choices over service providers, customers invest in the process. They, too, must focus on the outcome of finding a job in order to choose the best provider for their needs.

Our best hope for America's poor is to revitalize and empower the very institutions that welfare, for so long, displaced.

Public funds can help by providing transitional benefits and supporting people who have found jobs instead of paying people for two years who won't find work. We should ensure that they can make it to and from work and that they continue to receive health care, child care, and affordable housing. This is truly a hand up. While expensive in the short term, to the extent that transitional support helps people find jobs and get off welfare, it is a bargain.

A competitive delivery system accomplishes all these goals. In 1992 I met Peter Cove and Lee Bowes, founders of a for-profit job training firm called America Works, and invited them to Indianapolis in hopes of changing the culture of the welfare department. Unlike the welfare bureaucracy, America Works has a stake in helping people find a job—the company is fully paid only after a client works in a real job for six months. In addition to offering training courses in word processing and basic math skills, America Works teaches such things as how to prepare resumes, dress appropriately, show up on time, and go through job interviews. In short, America Works develops marketable character.

After the training, America Works sales people place candidates
in entry-level jobs. For a period of up to four months the individual's salary goes to America Works, which pays the employee
between $4.75 and $6.00 an hour, supplemented by a transportation subsidy and daycare provided by the welfare department. For
putting a welfare recipient back into the workforce, America
Works receives a $5,000 payment, part after four months of
employment and the rest after a successful six-month placement.
This is considerably less than the $13,000 a year government
spends on the average welfare recipient.

Approximately 95 percent of the people America Works places
are single mothers, a difficult segment of the population to place.
In three years America Works has placed five hundred people
locally and, since its founding in 1984, has placed fifteen thousand
nationally in lasting jobs.

At first, almost everyone complained when America Works
came to town. Other social service providers objected to a for-
profit company providing job training, indirectly suggesting that
profits and good deeds were mutually exclusive. They also complained about an out-of-state company servicing the poor, and the
bureaucracy howled about performance-based competition. Nevertheless, after we successfully forced America Works into the
mix, the rest of the system convulsed, and then demanded to be
allowed to compete. Today, the local job training council, the Private Industry Council, and to some extent (albeit grudgingly) the
welfare department, contract on a performance basis with many
different providers, and a true market for job training services
exists in Indianapolis.

Goodwill Industries of Central Indiana, an earlier foe of America Works, set out to be a first-rate competitor by developing
neighborhood-based partners and placing hundreds of individuals

in jobs. Another firm that helps move people from welfare to work is The Training Institute (TTI), which trains people to meet the needs of specific employers. TTI works in the tough Meadows area, designated as an Urban Enterprise Zone (an area that is a tax-haven for businesses) by federal and state authorities, providing training and placement only to recipients of food stamps or AFDC. The average pay for those placed by TTI is $7.12 an hour. TTI estimates that in its first year alone the company saved taxpayers $1.8 million by removing 110 people from the welfare rolls.

As in other areas of government where we have successfully broken up monopolies, the market has focused job training and placement efforts on customers—welfare recipients and other unemployed individuals seeking work. Competing companies recognize that different people respond to different strategies, and tailor their approaches to individual needs. Instead of government's one-size-fits-all solutions, to be successful these companies must be sensitive to the immense variety of problems experienced by those who must at one time or another apply for welfare. The resulting diversity of approaches gives these customers choices over what style works best for them.

Perhaps the greatest advantage of our market-based system of job training is that it allows us to take advantage of some of the strongest forces for good in troubled neighborhoods. In Indianapolis we contract with a number of neighborhood-based organizations to provide job training, and the same could be done in a competitive welfare system. When social services are provided through these organizations, case numbers become real people with real problems. These neighborhood-based providers are far better than government at integrating public assistance into an effort to rebuild families and discourage teenage pregnancy.

People who know the neighborhood and their clients replace impersonal big government programs. Some individuals are not prepared to work because they live with an abusive boyfriend, or are alcoholics, or have a very difficult son. Some people lack training and most lack confidence. Allowing neighborhood-based groups to fill this role helps rebuild the network of community support that welfare has eroded for the past thirty years.

Reestablishing the role of these groups within their communities has positive effects that reach far beyond reducing welfare rolls, helping to restore community ties and energizing area residents to confront common problems together.

The Care Center, a nonprofit organization closely affiliated with a local church, is one such organization in Indianapolis. Cramped into a ninety-year-old former school building, the Care Center provides health care, shelter for the homeless and battered, counseling, child care, a kitchen, and a food pantry. The director of the center, Ernie Medcalfe, says he would be interested in contracting to provide social services, because the Care Center's stabilizing influence in the neighborhood, its network through the church, and its understanding of the particular needs of the poor families in its neighborhood would make it a much better provider than government. He thinks he can do a superior job finding work for his neighborhood's welfare recipients and providing them with the support to keep working. And he is right. There are thousands of institutions like the Care Center in troubled neighborhoods across America. We chatter about welfare reform while allowing these resources to go untapped.

In the end, we need to recognize that the best way to reduce poverty is by creating marketable character—the ability and desire to get up every morning and go to work to support yourself and your family. Welfare destroyed this value; we must now restore it.

The most effective means is a strong network of support within poor communities. Active neighborhood organizations, vibrant communities of faith, and, most importantly, strong families are absolutely necessary to teach young adults about the importance of education, to prevent teen pregnancy, and to provide support for those experiencing hardship. Our best hope for America's poor is to revitalize and empower these very institutions that welfare displaced for so long.

Chapter Eight

Education

When I graduated from Broad Ripple High School in 1964, enrollment in the Indianapolis Public Schools system (IPS) topped one hundred thousand. By 1997 it was less than fifty thousand. Enrollment declined because parents exercised school choice the old-fashioned way: they moved.

A letter I received from "a tired IPS parent" diagnosed the situation well. She wrote:

> People with greater economic resources will always have a choice to escape to outlying school districts or private schools. But who will choose to live within the old city limits if the school system is always fraught with chaos? The inner city will continue to decline and will be faced with further decay.

Parents with school-age children are not the only ones leaving urban areas because of public school problems. Skyrocketing taxes affect everyone. More than any other service, education drives the growth of big-city taxes. Residents of Indianapolis are usually shocked when they learn that approximately 44 percent of their property tax dollar goes to the school system, 21 percent funds the city's police and fire departments, and 9 percent funds everything else city government does.

The economic effect of failing schools is dramatic. Real estate agents tell me the first question asked by prospective home buyers is almost always about the public school system, and city planners tell me that at the edge of the district, homes outside the IPS district sell quicker and for more money than homes on the other side of the street, located inside the district.

The academic performance of IPS students, like those of children in most urban districts, is intolerably poor. Barely half of the students graduate. More than 80 percent of the system's eighth graders failed Indiana's basic skills exam in 1995. At Broad Ripple, one of the best-performing high schools in the system that year, two-thirds of the students failed the basic skills test in language. Nearly a quarter of IPS students failed the test completely and qualified for summer remediation.

The usual response from defenders of the school system is that urban school districts such as IPS must deal with children who are harder to teach. While there is certainly some truth to this, it does not absolve the school system from responsibility. We compared the test results of students in IPS to the results of students in our inner-city Catholic schools, which have similar demographics. At St. Philip Neri, for example, the Catholic elementary school where I delivered my 1997 State of the City address, nearly three-quarters of the students are low-income and qualify for the federal school lunch program.

We found that the Catholic school second graders scored 1.3 points below the state average on the basic skills test; eighth graders, however, scored 1.4 points *above* the state average. Similarly, 9 percent of Catholic school second graders failed the basic skills test, while only 4 percent of eighth graders failed the test.

Although our analysis was not a scientific study, it certainly appeared that the longer students are in a Catholic school, the better they do relative to the state average.

We cannot ignore that public schools are failing to prepare their students to succeed in the twenty-first century economy.

IPS students, on the other hand, seemed to perform worse every year they were in the system. IPS second graders scored 8.5 points behind the state average, with 13 percent failing the test completely. IPS eighth graders fell to 15.4 points below the state average, and the number of students failing completely rose to 21 percent.

There is nevertheless no question that some individual schools in IPS, and in urban school systems across the country, do a terrific job educating children. During a recent visit to School 44, an outstanding school in a difficult neighborhood, a class of fourth graders greeted me in Japanese as their teacher looked on with pride.

But we cannot ignore that public schools on the whole are failing to prepare their students to succeed in the twenty-first century economy. The Indianapolis Private Industry Council estimated in 1997 that there were nearly twenty thousand jobs open in the Indianapolis metropolitan area. I talk with executives each month who complain about the shortage of qualified labor, and I know that many businesses resort to recruiting workers from Mexico and beyond. Yet thousands of Indianapolis residents remain unemployed. We have a mismatch between jobs and qualifications that only education can correct.

When education bureaucrats complain that I am too critical of the IPS system, I show them a 1993 article from the *Indianapolis Star* that tells the story of a mother who gave up guardianship of her daughter so the girl could escape the IPS system. After first keeping her daughter home for three weeks and running afoul of truancy laws, the mother had guardianship transferred to her eldest son and his family, who lived across town in a better school district.

When parents give up their children to avoid the public school system, then government has failed in its responsibility. Our imperative to change the system becomes more than economic; it becomes moral.

Like most mayors, I have no authority over schools. I have spent five years trying to make an impact on the system in every way imaginable. I pressured the districts publicly not to raise taxes, with little effect. I lobbied unsuccessfully for state legislation to create publicly funded vouchers and charter schools. I negotiated with private education providers such as the Edison Project and Educational Alternatives, Inc., to open schools in Indianapolis. When all of these avenues failed, I created a bipartisan political action committee called the Alliance for Quality Schools to support reform candidates for the IPS school board. And when that did not accomplish all we hoped, I authored reform legislation giving the district broad powers to hold schools more accountable. The Indiana General Assembly passed the bill, but results have been slow in coming.

In short, I have probably notched more unsuccessful attempts to improve education than any mayor in America, a distinction I wear with honor. Two things are clear to me from these efforts. The first—and this is not a new observation—is that the best, and maybe only, hope for improvement is to break up the government monopoly on public education and allow competition to force improvement and innovation. There is no reason to believe urban schools will reform themselves without competition.

Second, we must blow up central rule-driven bureaucracies and allow individual schools to change. Our schools are filled with good teachers and principals who are trapped in bad systems. Liberating them is just as important as allowing school choice.

In other words, we must deregulate both the demand for education through school choice, and the supply of education through empowering teachers and principals at individual schools. Either alone is insufficient.

Breaking the Monopoly

The arguments in favor of vouchers and other school choice programs have been articulated well and are by now familiar to most. I will not add much to this debate, other than to echo its importance.

For me, the best crystallization of the need to inject competition came, perhaps not surprisingly, from Milton Friedman. I had the pleasure of spending some time with the Nobel Laureate economist and asked him what we could do to improve our public schools.

When I began, "Dr. Friedman, I would like to talk about public schools," he politely stopped me. "They are not *public* schools," he said quickly. "They are *government* schools." Public, he explained, meant open to anyone. The schools to which I referred were government schools.

Not yet grasping the magnitude of what Friedman was saying, I continued as if he had made a semantic point, interesting but hardly of paramount importance to the general discussion. But he persevered. "Quit trying to reform the government schools," he said, "they are a monopoly. The only thing that will reform a monopoly is competition."

"Innovation," he went on, "derives from markets, and markets come from customers. If you do not have customers, you do not have markets. And if you do not have markets, you cannot have innovation." Because the school system is a monopoly, the customers—parents who want the best for their children—have little impact. We will not see any improvement in the nation's woefully inadequate system of government schools until parents become customers. After our experiences breaking up government monopolies in other services, this conclusion resonated with our general philosophy.

Parents could have some choice today if public school monopolies would simply let parents select the government-operated school they prefer. Pilot projects in Michigan and elsewhere provide this opportunity, granting parents the chance at least to opt out of particularly bad individual schools.

Vouchers allow some school funding to follow the child, which provides true purchasing power to the parent and allows the family to select the school of its choice, whether public, private, or religious. Vouchers can be funded with public dollars, as has been tried in Milwaukee and Cleveland, or they can be private, as in Indianapolis.

Indianapolis is fortunate to be the home of one of the country's most effective private voucher programs. The Choice Charitable Trust was created in 1991 by Pat Rooney, founder of Golden Rule Insurance Company. Each year, the Choice Trust raises almost $750,000 to fund scholarships to private schools for inner-city Indianapolis children. The scholarships cover up to half of the tuition at any private school, not to exceed $800. More than two-thirds of parents in the program choose their neighborhood Catholic school. The program currently funds 1,014 scholarships, with 650 students on the waiting list.

As a member of the board, I attended an annual picnic for students and their families. I heard marvelous stories. Parents were finally able to find a safe, good school that stimulated their children. They radiated pride in the schools and in the students. Critics argue that voucher programs such as the Choice Trust succeed because they take the best students from the public schools. Interestingly, my casual conversations with parents of more than one child contradicted that claim. When unable to send both children to private schools, these parents were much more likely to use the scholarships for children performing poorly, not those who were thriving in the public schools.

> I have probably notched more unsuccessful attempts to improve education than any mayor in America, a distinction I wear with honor.

Harder evidence of the effectiveness of these vouchers came from a study performed for the Choice Trust by the Hudson Institute, an Indianapolis-based think tank. Hudson researchers compared the performance of students who received Choice scholarships with the performance of students on the waiting list, thus presumably controlling for the influence of parental involvement. Students who received the Choice grants consistently outperformed their counterparts in IPS.

Even if we were to throw away every study showing that students in private schools perform better than students from comparable backgrounds in public schools, there would still be a compelling reason to allow school choice: the people who rely on public schools to educate their children want it. When I formed the Alliance for Quality Schools to recruit and support candidates for the IPS school board in 1994, we conducted extensive polling of school district residents. Our poll showed that respondents favored vouchers by a two-to-one margin, with support reaching 80 percent among African American women.

The most popular argument against vouchers is that they allow the better students to leave the system, leaving the remaining students worse off. I have always found this logic perverse. Arguing that we should use the power of the state to trap some children in poorly performing schools in order to protect other students is at least unfair if not simply bizarre.

First, parents can define what is in their children's best interest better than bureaucrats, and therefore by definition vouchers make a large segment of the population better off immediately. Second, most voucher programs actually increase per-pupil spending for the remaining students, because the public schools continue to be reimbursed in some amount for students who leave the school. For example, in IPS per-pupil expenditures are almost $8,000. Allowing $2,500 to follow a student would both help that student and increase funding for the remaining students by $5,500. And most important, everything we have done in Indianapolis convinces us that competition would make all schools perform better.

How can the public schools continue to oppose voucher programs and other reforms in the face of public opinion? Not only do public schools insulate themselves from customers, they often also protect themselves from voters. Like many urban school districts, IPS elects its school board members during primary elections, when fewer people vote. As an extra safeguard against public opinion, board members are elected by paper ballot, the only office so elected in Indianapolis, and voters at many polling sites must specifically ask for a ballot. Taken together, these factors dramatically suppress voter participation in school board elections. In a district with more than 350,000 residents, fewer than 12,000 votes can win an at-large seat on the school board and 3,000 votes can win a seat in one of the 5 districts. Given that the system itself employs nearly 5,000 people with a vested interest in the status quo, the ability of poor parents to secure change through the ballot box is virtually nil. Los Angeles Mayor Richard

Riordan calls the election of school board members by district one of the greatest impediments to school reform.

Deregulating Supply

Creating a market for education means more than just allowing choices. It means creating a wide range of schools for parents to choose from. If all schools look alike, then choice is meaningless. Every year administrators debate whether schools should stress the basics, offer magnet programs, feature certain teaching styles, create K-8 education, or establish year-round schools. The answer should be an emphatic yes to all. Every child learns differently, and the best results occur when parents can choose the type of school that best fits their child's needs. Systems should allow an explosion of creativity by individual schools and let results and parental preference shape the marketplace.

This point was made clear to me during a visit to an IPS school in 1994. At the time, IPS operated a limited public school choice program called "Select Schools," which allowed parents to choose the public school their children attended as long as all the schools remained within court-ordered racial balances.

The school I visited on that day was described in its Select Schools brochure as having school uniforms and a science magnet program. As a gracious vice principal took me through the school, I noticed that virtually none of the children was wearing a uniform. Since the administrator seemed perfectly at ease, a growing emperor-has-no-clothes feeling began to grow in me. Finally, I couldn't take it any longer and asked whether I was perhaps mistaken about the policy.

The administrator explained that since not every student was there by choice, the school felt it could only encourage uniforms, not require them. Not surprisingly, few students participated. I should not have been surprised a few moments later when I asked students in one classroom to name their favorite subject. Music, gym, English, and others all got votes—but not one hand went up for science, the school's magnet program.

When I retold that story in Indianapolis, the teachers' union reacted with "there-you-go-again:" blaming everything on teachers. Far from it! The teachers and administrators at that school were being asked to compete for students without being given the ability to change their product. Without the ability to reallocate resources to science equipment, or the freedom to require uniforms, the teachers and administrators were in a no-win situation.

I received a letter from an IPS teacher in 1993 that is one of the best summaries of this point. The teacher wrote:

> Pick up any case study from anywhere in our country and you will find that the only successful school reform comes from the grassroots level. Communities and teachers left to create and make their own decisions on how to improve students' academic growth are the only documented process of success.
>
> This community must also trust and free the teachers of this school system to do what is right, to use our intimate knowledge of our students to create a program of success.
>
> All of us, especially those in power to create change, must see that the teachers and students of IPS are losing control and power over their destinies on a daily basis. As money and power move farther and farther from the classroom our fate is sealed for the worst.

Charter schools are the most obvious way to allow innovation at the individual school level. Charter schools are exempted from most regulations except those concerning health and safety, but held strictly accountable for results. But what we should really aspire to is for every public school to have the freedoms currently being proposed for charter schools. Our thinking was influenced heavily by the excellent work of the Manhattan Institute in the field of school-based innovation. Sy Fliegel's *Miracle in East Harlem* (1993), which recounts the remarkable success of Harlem's District Four in creating innovative choices for parents, is a must read for all local officials.

> **Our only hope for improvement is to break up the government monopoly on public education and allow competition to force improvement and innovation.**

Our experience in moving Indianapolis city services into the marketplace revealed that our employees feared competition in part because they were locked into a system that stifled discretion, rewarded tenure instead of performance, was thick with middle managers, and provided no authority at the front-line level. Sound like a school system? Consider how the same strategic tools that allowed city employees to accomplish remarkable results would allow schools to innovate and compete, starting with activity-based costing.

Nowhere is the belief that more government spending produces better results more entrenched than in education. Despite a mountain of evidence to the contrary, the notion still remains that higher taxes for education will lead to a better quality product. I got a first-hand glimpse of how strongly people hold this belief when I unintentionally became involved in the debate over a tax increase proposed by the Washington Township school district. Washington Township is the wealthiest of the city's nine townships. A controversial antitax activist named Ann Hanley protested the tax increase and sought my support. Committed to keeping taxes low, but respecting the authority of the school board, I wrote a letter to the superintendent encouraging the district to look for alternative sources of revenue, and commented to a reporter that I hoped the district would reconsider.

What I believed had been minimal intervention created a firestorm. The morning the story appeared, angry parents actually confronted my chief of staff Anne Shane in her driveway as she left for work, and upbraided her for our stand against school taxes. My former campaign manager, Mike Wells, whose children attended one of the schools scheduled for renovation, called me after parents and school officials begged him to intervene.

We presented literature demonstrating that there was no connection between money spent on education and the results achieved. We talked about alternative ways of financing improvements. But analytical discussion was impossible. To parents of children in the school system, the equation was simple: the schools needed improvements, and that meant more taxes.

The numbers consistently belie that assumption. Every year, urban school budgets go up. Every year, urban enrollment goes down. It does not take a math major to figure out that per-pupil expenditures are going through the roof. Yet every week the school boards are embroiled in a new debate over cutting programs. Like most government entities, schools almost never have a real feel for how much it costs them to provide their various services. By using activity-based costing, principals would see where every dollar was being spent within their school. Noninstructional services would be exposed as drains on the central mission, and layers of bureaucracy would suddenly become costs. Imagine what would happen if individual principals could choose whether to purchase the services of the central school administration—or spend the money on whatever promotes the mission of their school.

Rigorous costing would help schools focus on their core service. Schools ought to be in the business of educating kids. They do not need to be in the business of running school buses, mopping school floors, fixing school lunches, or any of the other noninstructional services that divert attention from the core business of education.

Attempting to put a percentage on the amount of money that actually makes it into the classroom is itself a political argument, but we estimate the figure in Indianapolis to be about thirty cents out of every dollar. Opening up noninstructional services, such as transportation, janitorial services, and food services, would produce millions of dollars in every major school district that could be spent on technology, supplies, and even teachers' salaries.

Performance measures would force fascinating conversations. Until our reform bill passed in 1995, it was illegal in Indiana to evaluate teachers, even partially, based on the academic performance of their students—even if the measurement was based on improvement instead of raw test scores. Predictably, our effort to do so met enormous resistance from the teachers' union.

Like government managers, teachers' unions often resist performance standards with the popular claim that "You really can't measure what we do." Our experience has shown that if you do not have clearly specified outcomes and measure performance based on them, "you're just practicing," as Mitch Daniels said. Our children deserve better than that. If the academic performance of students is not an accurate measure of teacher performance, we should ask what is and come to some agreement. What we should not do is agree that there is simply no way to distinguish good teachers and teaching practices from bad.

How about an educational equivalent of popular budgets? For the education marketplace to work effectively, parents need good information. Schools should publish and mail to parents annual reports of test scores, a description of agreed-upon performance measures and the school's success in meeting them, and a complete breakdown of costs. How quickly the education debate would change to focusing on results, not spending!

But the most important strategic tool is employee empowerment. Many people would be amazed at how little power dedicated school administrators have to upgrade their product under the current monopoly situation. During one of my school visits, a high school teacher made some disparaging remark about a dull textbook. When I asked her why she continued to use the book, she gave me a shocked look and explained that she had no control over books or curriculum. Subsequently, I would come to know that shocked look well. It really was one of helplessness, a look that said that the official has no authority. It was the same look I got when I asked a principal who was complaining about some of her teachers why she kept them. She said that she had no choice—she had not hired them, nor could she fire them. Even a superintendent confided that he had promoted several incompetent teachers to administrative positions because he could not fire them and he wanted to get them away from children.

An enormous good could result from changes in the management and organizational culture of public schools. In cooperation with the superintendent of IPS, I lobbied the legislature for a law that would allocate funds directly to schools, bypassing several layers of educational bureaucracy. The law gave schools much more authority, with budgeting and spending functions moved to the schoolhouse level. Principals would have the authority to spend funds in the manner they felt most effective and could exercise the right to purchase their support services within the system or outside it.

In hopes of changing the education dialogue to one that focused on results, the law encouraged school boards to adopt standards for performance and offer bonuses to teachers who exceeded these standards. In poorly perform-ing schools that did not improve after three years, the superintendent could declare the school in academic receiver-ship and override the collective bargaining contract on all but pay issues, providing substantial authority to create change.

> **In order to prepare our children for the challenges of the twenty-first century, parents must have choices over the schools their children attend.**

Alas, the school board, under pressure from timid bureaucrats, anxious principals, and tough unions, eroded much of the super-intendent's authority.

Oddly enough, the teachers' union fought tooth and nail against my proposals to give their members more authority and the opportunity to earn bonuses (even without the risk that any teacher would earn less). The union's arguments against the pro-posals made no reference to their possible impact on education. Instead, their attacks centered on work rules for teachers.

The Inalienable Right

Opposed to any form of competition—particularly from private organizations—the teachers' union was enraged when I encour-aged Educational Alternatives, Inc., a private company that man-ages public schools, to do business in Indianapolis. Using a classic bureaucratic argument, they asked incredulously how I could even think of allowing a corporation to make a profit educating children. The presumption seemed to be that only selfless government bureaucrats could actually perform good deeds. According to the teachers' union, profit by definition meant exploitation.

A conversation in my office with union officials about these for-profit schools brought the issue of government monopolies full circle. Offering a compromise, I agreed to stop lobbying for private charter schools for three years, if the union would support the creation of a charter school run by a group of IPS teachers.

The union's response? "Over our dead bodies!" In my office that day, the union stated categorically that it would never agree to any proposal that used incentives, rewarded performance, or allowed any group of teachers to operate under rules different from any other.

This is the same response we would have received from city workers if they had possessed veto rights over whether they would compete in the marketplace. But they didn't. Although today competition has allowed those workers to earn more, produce more, and enjoy greater autonomy, they would never have abandoned the status quo for the uncertainty of the marketplace unless forced. They rose to the challenge of competition because they had to in order to stay in business.

The teachers' union, on the other hand, perhaps the most powerful political body in Indiana, does have what amounts to a veto on legislative change. As long as our teachers' union and others like it across the country choose to protect the government education monopoly, our schools will continue to produce a standard monopolistic product—poor results at high costs. That is why vouchers are so important.

To prepare our children for the challenges of the twenty-first century, parents must have choices over the schools their children attend. There is no substitute, and there is no justification for denying parents what should be an inalienable right.

The diversity of good schools needs to increase as well— through more private schools as well as charter schools. And of course we must liberate public schools. A few years ago during a visit to School 111, an elementary school on the city's southeast side, I met an energetic group of teachers and their committed principal, Honey Poole. They wanted to charter their own school. These intrepid teachers created their own self-study course in charter schools, and developed ideas for teaching methods, curriculum, and budgeting. Teachers like the ones at School 111 are the hope for urban school districts, and there are thousands of them across the country. Our challenge is to liberate parents and teachers from the bureaucratic monopoly of government schools, and let them create a thriving diversity of good schools.

Chapter Nine

Crime and Community

I have ridden with police officers a few times a year for twenty years. As prosecutor, I personally handled a dozen death penalty cases, as well as countless cases of rape, child abuse, and robbery. My deputies and I prosecuted four hundred thousand cases in twelve years and sent more people to prison than anyone in Indiana history. Yet nothing prepared me for the casual lawlessness I saw on a ride I took in 1992.

That night I accompanied several officers in their work on our near north side, an area sandwiched in the two-and-a-half miles that separated our revitalized downtown and the stable middle-class neighborhoods to the north. I challenged one of the young officers to show me a drug deal. The officer turned the corner toward 29th and Talbot, and told me the name of the dealer we were going to see and what he would be selling. When the dealer saw the officer, he lumbered up the steps to the porch, more as a cavalier effort to sit down than to escape. When I asked the officer why he did not arrest the dealer, he replied that he had done so several times that month. Next I suggested that we use the legal system to confiscate the house from which the dealer operated. The officer explained that it was not the dealer's house, but the house of an innocent person the dealer had intimidated.

More to appease me than out of any confidence that he had solved a problem, the officer made the arrest. A wagon picked up the prisoner, and our ride continued. Block by block the story was repeated, with groups of young men brazenly dealing drugs in full public view. Open criminal activity had become the norm.

Indianapolis has always been one of the safest large cities in America, but during the 1990s the face of crime changed in Indianapolis, just as it did all over the country. Crack cocaine hit Indianapolis like a tornado. When I left my job as prosecutor in 1990, only 22 percent of arrested felons tested positive for the drug. A scant four years later, 70 percent of offenders registered positive for cocaine at the time of their arrest. The impact of crack on the nature of crime is unprecedented. It is cheap, easy to get, and highly addictive. Young mothers prostitute themselves to obtain it, and appallingly young children participate in its sale. Wherever crack is found, violence is widespread, vicious, and completely irrational.

Around 1994 our city received the full brunt of crack-related violence. The homicide rate, essentially unchanged for two decades, finally started to spiral out of control. The police tried everything—saturating neighborhoods with patrols, aggressively stopping suspicious cars, even copying highly successful programs used in New York and Boston to reduce the murder rate—but still the drug murders continued. Other large cities had already watched their murder rates double in the wake of crack before they eased. In Indianapolis, the increase was just beginning.

Concurrently, the institutions that help individuals resist crime and impulse—family, religion, peers, and role models—also broke down. The collapse of the family, for example, contributed to an increase in violent crimes. Fatherlessness created a new breed of young offender, angrier and more vicious than his predecessor. An analysis by Heritage Foundation scholars (*Backgrounder*, March 17, 1995) indicates that a 10 percent increase in the percentage of children living in single-parent homes typically leads to a 17 percent increase in juvenile crime. Even in high-crime inner-city neighborhoods, well over 90 percent of children from safe, stable homes do not become delinquents. *By contrast only 10 percent of children from unsafe, unstable homes in these neighborhoods avoid crime.*

As middle-class residents moved from inner-city neighborhoods, and more young men and women dropped out or were kicked out of school, gangs became the primary institution in many areas. A sea change occurred, and the police, community, and courts needed to make big changes.

Police and the Community

During my twelve years as prosecutor, I watched as tension grew between the police department and urban residents. The "rapid response" policing practiced for most of the past twenty years emphasized quick responses to 911 calls, but did not promote public confidence in the police department. Residents saw officers drive into an area quickly, make an arrest, and leave. One veteran police officer described it this way:

When I came on the job, we'd patrol an area out here, and there was no interaction with the public. They'd wave at us, but they'd wave at us with one finger. There was an occupying army kind of attitude toward the police. We'd go on a run, you'd be involved in an altercation with somebody you were trying to arrest, and that was the Saturday night entertainment. People would literally bring the grill out and start flipping burgers on the porch because this was fun, to watch police fight.

Neighborhood meetings in center city areas often turned nasty, as residents complained about police conduct and indifference to law-abiding members of the community. Faith in the criminal justice system eroded as people complained more about the police conduct than about criminal activity.

Rapid response policing took its toll on officers as well, alienating them from the people they served. With an emphasis on speed, officers left their cars only to make arrests, thus making most of their experiences in high-crime areas difficult and adversarial. Not surprisingly, many officers began to assume the worst of all residents in troubled neighborhoods, and often behaved accordingly. Even the best street officers tended to generalize when discussing people in certain sections of the city.

Neighborhood activist Violet Gwin described the problem well:

> Ninety-five percent of the people that the police officers meet are murderers, pedophiles, burglars, and people like that. They don't run into people like you and me. They don't have to deal with me. They don't hear me say, "Officer, how are you? Let me buy you a cup of coffee." Why? Because I'm just not always around them because they're always dealing with murderers and that type of thing.

The resulting conflicts created a gulf between the police department and the law-abiding residents they were protecting. And just as law enforcement was breaking down, the situation got much worse with the appearance of crack cocaine.

Rapid-response policing would never provide enough force to fight the effects of crack without the support of the community. A new vision of policing, one that joined the community and police in a mutually supportive partnership, was required.

The restructuring of the Indianapolis Police Department proved the most painful battle of my political life.

We needed to go beyond merely arresting people; we needed to actually prevent crime. Police officers needed to do more than patrol communities; they had to become part of them, as indeed they used to be.

We found the answer in the idea of community policing. As a Research Fellow in Criminal Justice at Harvard's Kennedy School of Government, I saw firsthand the pioneering work of Mark Moore and George Kelling, who along with James Q. Wilson developed the theory of community policing. According to Moore, community policing means two things: bringing police and citizens into working partnerships, and giving the police responsibility for identifying and solving neighborhood problems.

Managing the Cultural Change

Under the traditional management approach, in most urban police departments, authority is centralized at department headquarters. The department views itself as a paramilitary operation, emphasizing rank and order instead of problem-solving by teams. Promotions are based largely on tests, and paperwork takes precedence over patrol. To the extent that performance is measured, it is often based more on how quickly an officer reaches the scene of the crime than on what the officer does when he or she gets there.

Community policing requires police departments to make significant changes in management, training, and deployment. It is critically important that authority and discretion be given to those in the front lines, to the street officers. The beat officer has to become the most important figure in the department.

Kelling and other advisors counseled me to implement the change slowly, insisting that such a major shift in police culture would take years to bring about. Too much pressure would produce a backlash in the department, while too little would slow much-needed changes.

Like most mayors, my authority over the police department was severely limited. Mayors can choose the police chief and the deputy chiefs, but they cannot hire, fire, demote, or promote any individual officers. In Indianapolis, if a chief comes from inside the department, when he or she is replaced he or she stays with the rank of captain and remains part of the culture. Management and beat officers all belong to the same union, forging virtually impenetrable solidarity.

Policing More and Better

Putting more officers on the street will not stop crime, but it sure helps. Even as we cut the budget and reduced the city workforce as a whole, our competition initiative in other areas allowed us to invest an additional $100 million in public safety over five years.

We defined an hour spent on the street as more valuable than an hour spent on paperwork at headquarters. Determined to drive the number of hours on the street as high as possible, I asked the chief to look at the work of the street officers, hour by hour, and identify functions that resulted in neither arrests nor in time spent with the community. We paid particular attention to activities such as taking accident reports, dusting for fingerprints, transporting prisoners and stolen property, directing traffic, and much more.

Under the existing rapid response system, radios and cars had a lock on the department. The 911 dispatch system often sent officers scurrying in response to nonemergency calls. People called to file reports for insurance purposes, to check the vehicle identification numbers on cars they were buying, to complain about graffiti, and hundreds of other minor matters. During an hour I spent working with 911 dispatchers, one caller falsely claimed a medical emergency in order to get an item picked up from the pharmacy.

Changing our goal from beating the clock to increasing public safety required better use of police hours. We began to divert non-emergency calls to specially trained civilians, saving hundreds of runs a day. The Public Safety Officer program began using civilians to handle a range of other activities, from transporting prisoners to investigating accidents. We moved officers out of headquarters and into the districts, and maximized the time they could spend on patrol. These strategies resulted in a 20 percent increase in available street strength, without additional dollars.

Technology also produced smarter, more effective community policing. Police received take-home cars, each with a computer. The system allowed officers to access crime and vehicle databases while on patrol. Police management expert Lawrence Sherman helped create a system wherein each officer could receive and analyze crime data block by block within a precinct.

Officers used the sophisticated crime data to meet with neighbors and map out solutions to tough problems. One such idea would come to be called the Safe Streets program. Local leaders asked the department to immerse tough areas in patrols and encouraged aggressive action, including stopping vehicles for traffic violations and questioning suspicious pedestrians.

We used a mapping approach refined by Police Commissioner Bill Bratton in New York and, after charting high-crime areas and high-crime times, asked the police to make every legal pedestrian and vehicle stop that they could during those times. In the first month of the program, police spent 3,700 hours on 5,268 vehicle stops, resulting in 4,302 citations, 98 felony arrests, 662 misdemeanors arrests, and 127 gun and drug seizures.

Residents responded enthusiastically, saying that for the first time in months they felt safe using their front porch and walking to the corner.

Protecting Public Areas and Repairing Broken Windows

Early in my administration, I had a conversation with Mayor Richard Daley of Chicago, who related with great pride two of his favorite achievements: the speed with which Chicago now towed abandoned cars and a new silicone-based paint that made it easy to remove grafitti. Initially it struck me as strange that of all the terrific things occurring in Chicago, the mayor chose to boast about these seemingly small accomplishments. But Mayor Daley's anecdotes later proved instructive. Abandoned cars and graffiti send negative signals about a neighborhood's importance to city government, and they can even promote crime.

The need to cure problems like these was enunciated by George Kelling and James Q. Wilson in 1982 when they introduced the concept of "Broken Windows" (*Atlantic* magazine, 1982) policing with the following description:

A stable neighborhood of families who care for their homes, mind each others' children, and confidently frown on unwanted intruders can change, in a few years or even a few months, to an inhospitable and frightening jungle. A piece of property is abandoned, weeds grow up, a window is smashed. Adults stop scolding rowdy children; the children, emboldened, become more rowdy. Families move out, unattached adults move in. Teenagers gather in front of the corner store. The merchant asks them to move; they refuse. Fights occur. Litter accumulates. People start drinking in front of the grocer's.

Disorder serves as a precursor for crime and is linked more closely to crime than other characteristics of the area, including poverty. Kelling notes that muggers and robbers "believe they reduce their chances of being caught or even identified if they operate on streets where potential victims are already intimidated by prevailing conditions" (*Fixing Broken Windows*, 1996).

New York Mayor Rudy Giuliani acted on Kelling's observations with impressive results. The department increased arrests for small offenses, clearing public spaces of disruptive conduct. Today not only are subways and street corners safer, but also the city's violent crime rate has plummeted.

We decided to eliminate our "broken windows" as quickly as possible. Officers reported problems they noted on patrol, looked for dangerous buildings or abandoned garages where assaults might occur, and suggested solutions. The Department of Public Works began the Graffiti Busters program, which allowed for the rapid removal of unsightly defacement and obscene scribblings.

Even seemingly small matters make a difference. For example, during one ride-along, an excellent officer asked a small favor. She lived in an area where drug traffic and loitering centered on a particular corner. Worrying about her young child, she thought that putting a street light on the corner would dispel the trouble. Six months after the city installed that light, the officer returned to express her gratitude and said that, as she had hoped, the light had caused the young men to move off the corner.

In 1993 a conversation with an elderly resident of a troubled neighborhood brought home the extent to which buildings that give shelter to illegal activity can undermine a neighborhood. The woman told me that she could not let her grandson out on the sidewalk in front of her house because the dealers in the neighboring crack house pressured the boy to run errands for them. She kept him all but imprisoned in the house to protect him from dealers who roamed the street freely. Society had turned upside down.

Throughout many low-income neighborhoods, buildings—vacant and occupied—give refuge to crimes, ranging from prostitution and drug dealing to underage alcohol consumption. Not only do these buildings facilitate criminal activity, but they are also highly visible symbols of community helplessness and the impotence of the criminal justice system.

An article by Tucker Carlson that appeared in *Policy Review* (Winter, 1995) demonstrates this clearly through the story of one Washington, DC, resident's attempts to drive a crack house out of the neighborhood:

> Conner and his neighbors repeatedly told police and the local vice squad about the crack houses, but to little effect. What Conner and his neighbors saw as a threat, the police considered just another crack house, and a relatively unimportant one. The drug dealers on Conner's block were active enough to disturb life in the

neighborhood, but not enough to interest the vice squad....

Looking back, Conner says he and his neighbors may have put too much confidence in local law enforcement. "The police do not view their job as shutting down a house like this," he says. "They view their job as arresting people." As Conner explains it, arresting dealers will not

The juvenile justice system has collapsed and no longer works for young offenders.

solve the problem. "As long as the buyers know to come there, somebody else will replace this guy if they put him in jail, and that's the reason that the whole house needs to be gotten control of."

In Indianapolis police and community residents formed creative partnerships to rid neighborhoods of nuisances, from open-air drug markets and crack houses to improperly run liquor stores. We sought to take control of these properties and rehabilitate them not only to improve neighborhood safety and confidence, but also to lend respect and credibility to community policing. A select group of officers received complaints from neighborhood residents and street officers, and then brought every possible legal tool to bear on eliminating the nuisance. City attorneys brought actions to seize dozens of properties, and public health, fire, and police departments wrote citations for nuisances that violated city ordinances. The city demolished dilapidated buildings and deeded sound structures to community organizations. In the first two years of the project more than a hundred nuisance sites were corrected or conveyed to not-for-profit development corporations.

One particularly positive experience involved a house in the city's Meridian-Kessler neighborhood. The house, unoccupied and surrounded by tall weeds, was littered with needles, liquor bottles, and trash. Police made numerous arrests at the location, which on more than one occasion led to the recovery of stolen property. Under legal pressure from the city, the owner of the property deeded it over to the local community development corporation and it became part of a Habitat for Humanity project. As appreciative neighbors like Caroline Farrar, executive director of the Meridian-Kessler Neighborhood Association, noted, "Not only did this transfer of property increase the value of homes along Winthrop, it also made possible the development of the Children's Community Garden at the site of this abandoned and crime infested building."

Certain business establishments—liquor stores in particular— seem to be magnets for loitering, drug dealing, and other criminal conduct. Helping neighborhood groups combat these nuisances empowers and emboldens active community members.

The civilian member of our nuisance-fighting group, Marni Bader, has become something of a folk hero to neighborhood leaders. Through sheer tenacity she solved problems within months that had plagued communities for years. When Marni and others went after "500 Liquors," a center-city chain with a history of serious problems, the city provided her and others appearing before the licensing board with legal advice on how to get the store's license revoked. Working in conjunction with activist neighbors and other advocates, the new team forced several of the stores to close and the remainder to be sold to an owner who was more responsive to community concerns.

Late last year I was surrounded by cheering neighbors at an inner-city liquor store, long a serious neighborhood nuisance. The store, abutting a residential area, drew the lawless, drunks, and drug dealers and thus loudly proclaimed that criminals, not citizens with positive values, ruled the area. Surrounded by inner-city residents, community development leaders, pastors, and children, we announced the closure of the store. The store represented just one nuisance in a large area, but it was a highly significant sign in the battle for control of public spaces. Before friends and television cameras, the Reverend Jim Harrington, one of the leaders, praised God and thanked his friends that good had triumphed.

Partnerships that Worked

Captain Mike Elder is the role model for a new breed of IPD officer. His territory includes Clearstream Gardens, a public housing development which had the highest crime rate in Indianapolis before Elder drew the assignment. Working with other south district officers, Elder set up a community resource center at the housing complex to provide residents with a place where they could get help quickly. Many officers worked overtime, talking to tenants and collecting valuable information about problem areas and disruptive residents.

Elder convinced a neighborhood video store to donate movies to the center, and he began showing them for young people. The "movie house" gave children something safe to do and rapidly became a popular spot. Far from satisfied, Elder asked business and community groups to help renovate the Clearstream Gardens gym for sports and other youth activities. The gym provided a safe place for recreation and added a sense of community. Anyone caught committing a crime is banned from the facility, which keeps the location safe and, more importantly, serves as a deterrent and sends a message.

Others were so impressed with Clearstream's successes that they offered to help. The suburban Franklin Township Churches Association, for example, set up a mentoring program. Several member churches of the local African American Minister's Association adopted distressed families, providing guidance on budgets and teaching marketable job skills. The Marion County Health Department put in a new clinic that offered basic services such as preventative dentistry, and the Department of Parks and Recreation supplied staff to a summer program at Elder's Clearstream Gardens gym. Elder also reestablished a relationship with the mobile library—introducing children to books, which were once unattainable.

Thanks in no small part to Mike Elder's smart policing, police runs to Clearstream dropped from 1,500 in 1991 to 350 in 1994—a 74 percent decline. Today, residents cooperate with the police and give them tips that stop crime before it happens. The improved atmosphere is evident to the neighborhood. "Before Mike came in," says one Clearstream mother, "I didn't dare let my kids play outdoors because of the shootings and drug deals going down at all hours of the day and night. People living in projects want a normal life, too—and we're getting there."

Parkview Place Apartments is another success story. Parkview Apartments is a 185-unit housing complex for 650 people on the near north side of Indianapolis. A couple of years ago, bullets ricocheted throughout the complex. Drug deals, gunfire, shattered glass, and drunken brawls were part of daily life in Parkview. Sharon Williams, a resident for three years, was afraid to let her two children play there. "Every time my kids want to go out back to play, I have to go out back with them," Sharon complained. Another resident recalled, "If you came out, you could expect people to throw a bottle or a brick at your car. It was just completely out of control" (*Indianapolis News*, April 9, 1993).

On the evening of February 2, 1993, the Parkview apartment manager and a secretary were pistol-whipped, beaten, and robbed by five men. Following the robbery, we implemented a community policing project at Parkview to turn the situation around. The residents and managers of Parkview formed a partnership with the police and agreed to help them spot and solve problems from littering to drugs. Police officers immediately began regular meetings with Parkview Place management and the newly organized resident group. The department promised high visibility in the area through car and foot patrols, including frequent one-on-one interactions with people in the area. They used special IPD units in the area—traffic officers, mounted patrols, canines, helicopter patrols, and additional narcotics officers. Police also supported the hiring of private

> **Tolerating crime when it can be deterred benefits neither the criminal nor the community.**

security officers by the managers of the property after IPD and the citizens of Parkview strongly recommended additional help.

With help from the residents and management, the department developed a database of approximately two thousand reports from which dossiers were developed on problem addresses and persons. Information in the dossiers included criminal histories, mugshots, and information obtained from beat and narcotics officers.

Trespass laws were strictly enforced. People who were neither living in nor visiting anyone in the complex were trespassing and consequently removed. If they showed up again they were arrested. Management evicted tenants involved in criminal activity.

Changing traffic patterns also helped keep criminals at bay. Parkview's apartments were accessible through three feeder streets, making surveillance difficult and drug trafficking easy. In fact, the area saw so much drug trafficking that it was commonly referred to as a "drive-through McDonald's of dope." At the request of IPD and residents, Parkview management used concrete barricades to block two of the three entrances to the complex. Lillie Sales, a longtime resident of Parkview, says, "Since the barricades were put up we don't have a lot of drive-by shootings and you don't see any more of the gangs hanging around.... They don't have anything to hang around for" (*Indianapolis Recorder*, October 23, 1993). Adhering to the "broken windows" theory of policing, the IPD convinced Parkview management to undertake a number of small but important improvements, which included removing old and abandoned vehicles, improving lighting, repaving driveways, adding speed bumps, and installing large metal dumpsters to help control litter.

The improvement was dramatic. From first quarter 1993 to first quarter 1995, dispatched radio runs fell from 168 to 84; incidents requiring a police report fell from 108 to as low as 53; and aggravated assaults dropped from 14 to 0.

Listening to the residents shows the impact of the new-found community at Parkview:

> "For the past six months you wouldn't believe the turnaround out here," says Damon Johnson, a maintenance man and former resident of Parkview. "It was kind of scary because everyone had a pistol. People were scared to come out of their houses. People were scared to send their kids outside or send them to the bus stop by themselves because they didn't know what to expect. It's turned around a great deal due to the residents, the management, and IPD."

Or even more simply stated by resident Aaron Dill, "Things are different now, ain't nothing out here but some happiness" (*Indianapolis Recorder*, October 23, 1993).

Decriminalizing Crime

The arrest of Frank Colbert Williams for murdering Deidra L. Copeland says a lot about why containing crime is so difficult.

Williams had been arrested dozens of times and sentenced to the state correctional system twice. Juvenile Court Judge James Payne sent the hardened street thug to the state for safekeeping. Less than ninety days later he was released, and within thirty days murdered Ms. Copeland. Experts estimate that more than one-third of murders nationally are committed by convicted felons who have been released by courts and prison authorities.

Criminal justice researchers speak in terms of specific and general deterrence. The former deters a specific individual: if a person is in prison he may not be reformed but he cannot commit a crime outside the walls. The latter suggests that the prison sentence will deter others. The system does neither, because it does not keep offenders locked up and therefore does not deter crime. I frequently think back to one of my first habitual criminal trials, that of a professional thief named Tommy Wise. In these trials, after the defendant is found guilty of a crime, the jury reconvenes to hear evidence on whether the additional thirty-year sentence for habitual criminals should apply. Tommy fired his attorney between these stages of the trial on the reasonable grounds that he had not been doing too well. Tommy then walked up to the jury, and said quite candidly, "I'm a professional criminal, and I'm used to doing about six months. If I thought I'd have to do fifteen to thirty years, I'd never have committed this crime."

In other words, crime pays. Criminals know this, and neighbors see it. This hit home when I joined neighborhood children to paint a large fifty-foot mural celebrating great African American leaders and a commitment to peace. This mural, painted over a battle-scarred wall of gang graffiti, proclaimed:

Here on this corner a day before we began to paint,
a young man's life ended in a nightmare. This place is a
point of change, a place of remembering the dreams

that sleep in our hearts. Here on this corner, nightmares end and dreams begin. Dedicated to the dreams of our youth that they may live.

At the end of the unveiling ceremony an older man and his wife identified themselves as nearby residents. They asked why the city refused to evict the omnipresent crack dealers from the opposite corner. I turned to the street officer who had accompanied me to the mural dedication and asked him. He named two of the dealers, Michael Torrance and Timothy Brown, and claimed that he had repeatedly arrested them for a variety of charges. Upon returning to my office I asked for the dealers' criminal histories to check the officer's story. Michael and Timothy had survived three dozen arrests and were still out on the street.

The Juvenile Door Revolves More Quickly and With More Danger

Homicide investigators, corrections officials, and mothers of boys slain over minor slights all describe the complete amorality of the young adult, street-tough "superpredators." Neither respectful of life nor fearful of imprisonment, these young men destabilize neighborhoods and threaten citizens and cities alike—and there will be more of them, not fewer, in the next decade.

The clashes inside neighborhoods between older adults, who own property and care about their fellow citizens, and dangerous young adults beget anger and frustration. On a hot summer night in 1994 the police chief called me to 42nd and College on the city's north side. At a corner where we had invested millions in renovating buildings, dozens of young men were pelting officers with rocks and insults. The matter quickly escalated as more police generated more hostility. A total lack of respect for authority and property

could be seen on the faces of the protesters. Eventually, without too
much damage, the city's first disturbance in twenty years was over.
Over the next several days, I visited a wide range of neighborhood
residents. Older citizens demanded the more aggressive intervention
that had in part escalated the disturbance. Younger adults
demanded that the police
change their tactics and be more
tolerant. It soon became clear
that the city was experiencing a
battle between generations
rather than between races.

> **We proposed that the Indianapolis Police Department switch from a department that *responded* to crime to one that worked with the people to *prevent* crime.**

The juvenile justice system
has collapsed and no longer works for young offenders. Everybody knows this: the police who hate to waste their time going to
court, the offenders who get off without being forced to pay for
their crime, and the victims who are denied justice. The portrait of
the stern judge who guided children gone astray back to the right
path no longer applies. Street smart young men know how to play
the system with virtual impunity, and older criminals, knowing
these younger people face no punishment, routinely use them to
do the dirty work.

Auto theft and first-time business burglaries were practically
decriminalized for youths when they realized they would suffer no
consequences in committing the crimes. I still remember, when I
was a prosecutor, watching undercover tapes of an auto theft
sting. The adult seller of the vehicle bragged to our undercover
agent that he used juveniles to steal the cars because he knew that
if they were caught nothing would happen to them.

When crack cocaine hit and juvenile crimes grew by 400 percent, detention space increased by only 70 percent. The result of
course was that criminals served less time. The juvenile court was
a dumping ground for the communities' problems, but it was a

dump with limited capacity and few constructive alternatives. Prison officials, not the courts, decide how long juvenile felons will serve. These officials, concerned primarily with overcrowding, often undercut the good juvenile judges.

A Dozen Strikes and You're Out

More police officers, arresting the same criminals more times, is not a very effective solution. So the debate became whether tougher measures such as the "three strikes and you're out" legislation work. As prosecutor I used the Indiana equivalent of the law. To me, however, the debate was really over the Tommy Wise problem. As matters stand, the system imposes no sanctions when a young offender is the most violent and active, then imposes substantial penalties just as they are maturing and reaching the end of their high-crime years. Tommy and society would have been better served if he had received swift, certain punishment after each and every crime.

Right before the crack epidemic I asked the legislature to mandate penalties for cocaine. Indiana allows suspended sentences for small amounts and extraordinary sentences for larger amounts, but nothing in between. But the legislature and governor, worried about prison overcrowding, opposed mandatory minimum penalties.

States that have seen the largest decreases in crime are those with the largest increases in incarcerated criminals. Tolerating crime when it can be deterred benefits neither the criminal nor the community.

Neighborhood partnerships can make a difference here as well. Courtwatch programs help inform judges of the dire consequences of lenient sentences. Using police and prosecutor data, neighbors can monitor serious offenders, learn their court dates, and make their views known to the judge. A similar program established by

activist Glenna Chesser a few years ago evicted longtime prostitutes from the corners of a neighborhood that transitioned successfully from crime and decay to reasonable safety and
restoration. When Glenna appeared in court, the judges gave the
case and the offender added scrutiny (and time).

Communities Can Make a Difference

The violent youths I met during the episode on 42nd and College
reminded me how fragile cities are and how much havoc a few
really angry, amoral young adults can cause. Nevertheless:

- Community policing can help solve the problems that
  breed crime and encourage residents to fight back.
- Retaking public spaces and removing nuisances tell
  everyone that honest citizens are in control.
- Locking up violent offenders will reduce crime.

Community policing works when it gives law-abiding citizens
the confidence needed to set clear standards and participate as
partners with police in protecting their neighborhoods. Meaningful consequences for wrongful conduct reinforces the differences
between right and wrong for the community and for the criminal.

After four years of trying to reconnect the police and the community, something happened on March 13, 1997, that had an
enormous impact on our efforts to rebuild neglected areas. Presi-
dents of seven inner-city neighborhood associations representing
high-crime areas summoned me to the basement of Our Redeemer
Lutheran Church, located within a few blocks of the city's worst
crack-infested neighborhoods. Juanita Smith, who represented
one of the very toughest neighborhoods, presented me with a contract to sign. This extraordinary document spelled out what these

neighborhood leaders deemed necessary to make their streets safe again.

Remarkably, the contract offered by Juanita not only demanded more patrols and tougher judges but also accepted more responsibilities as well. The contract spelled out specific actions that she and her neighbors would undertake—photographing drug dealers, recording customers' license plates, and picketing problematic landlords—to support the police. These leaders wanted to work with officers to develop specific plans for reducing crime. They asked the city to live up to its responsibility, and they were willing to play an important role in that endeavor.

The police officers attending the meeting watched "their" residents with pride. For five years we had struggled to build community leadership in the fight against crime, and to convince the police that they needed the support of strong citizens to succeed, especially in tough areas. To us, this contract was clear evidence that the new approach had taken root.

Chapter Ten

Neighborhoods

We often think of inner cities as problems—areas to be feared, pitied, and assisted with government programs. This was the predictable result of mayors beseeching Washington for the better part of three decades, asking for more federal dollars because inner cities were awful, hopeless places.

As Northwestern University's John McKnight and John Kretzmann describe in a 1993 report "Mapping Community Capacity," looking at inner cities only as a collection of problems ignored their potential. This narrow perspective aggravated the situation by creating a culture of dependency within neighborhoods similar to the individual dependency created by welfare.

Given the desperate situation of our nation's inner cities, it is no surprise that most Americans think about lower-income urban neighborhoods as problems. Since these neighborhoods are noted for their deficiencies and needs, most elected officials codify and program them through deficiency-oriented policies and programs. Human services systems—often supported by foundations and universities—thereupon translate the programs into local activities that teach people the nature of their problems, and that services are the answer to these problems. As a result, many low-income urban neighborhoods are now service-oriented and believe that, being people with special needs, their well-being depends upon the goodwill of outsiders. Thus, gradually, they become mainly consumers with no incentive to be producers.

In the early 1990s, a new group of mayors emerged who rejected the deficiency-based approaches criticized by McKnight and Kretzmann. Mayor Norquist put it more simply when he said, "You can't build a city on pity." A new approach that focused on building wealth through the marketplace rather than redistributing it through social programs began to gain steam.

Increasingly, mayors recognized that poor neighborhoods had their own assets and competitive advantages that could be used to create growth. Professor Michael Porter, in an influential *Harvard Business Review* article, "The Competitive Advantage of the Inner City," (May/June 1995) encouraged cities to develop strategies based on inner-city assets such as their central location and available labor.

People who share my free market philosophy may find it difficult to accept that no matter how much we want to withdraw government from the marketplace, we cannot do it immediately. Poor communities have suffered so much from catastrophic government policies over the past thirty years that government is needed to undo the harm.

As Robert Woodson remarked in front of hundreds of neighborhood activists in a speech in Indianapolis:

> People on the political Right tend to believe that all we have to do is tear down the barriers to the free enterprise system, and let the survival of the fittest determine the winners and losers. But they fail to understand that participation in this market economy requires capital and requires information, which a lot of poor people don't have. People on the political Left tend to believe that even if poor people had the requisite information, they would still be too stupid to make informed decisions for themselves, so they need professionally trained people to make decisions for them.

Consider the difference I encountered when I walked through two new neighborhood developments in Indianapolis. Willowood, a gated community on the city's far north side, contained beautiful new $400,000 homes, immaculate new sidewalks and streets, and private security and trash pickup. The developer purchased the previously undeveloped area from a single owner and encountered no substantial zoning problems or remonstration. Homeowners in the development will send their children to high-quality public and private schools located nearby.

A few days later I visited Concord, an inner-city development in a working-class neighborhood known as Haughville. A dozen of the sixty units were finished, a mixture of duplexes and single-family dwellings that cost about $75,000 a unit. Fifty years ago, part of the site housed an industrial company that left materials now considered environmentally unsafe. Different persons owned various parts of the site, which was surrounded by decayed roads and curbs and several abandoned houses. Financial help from the federal Department of Housing and Urban Development brought its own set of rules, codes, and requirements, adding costs and slowing development. Children residing in the new area would be bused by federal court order to a school system many miles away. Crime was a major concern.

The city took a number of steps to address these challenges, providing environmental remediation, acquiring land, demolishing abandoned houses, repairing crumbling infrastructure, and increasing police patrols. City officials helped arrange financing for the project, and several neighborhood groups and public housing officials actively participated in planning. After three years of struggle, we all felt a great sense of pride over these wonderful new units.

Where the suburban site came about as the natural result of market forces, the inner-city site faced such significant obstacles that the marketplace alone would not have sparked the development. Through the active involvement of neighborhood organizations and the city, however, the project became viable, producing the first new housing units in the area in years.

We cannot simply pull out of communities destroyed by poor services and unwise welfare state intervention. But government's involvement must take a new form, fostering market-produced prosperity instead of making income transfers through welfare. First, government must do right by its basic responsibilities—safety, schools, and infrastructure. Second, government needs to help remove the structural barriers to investment by helping reduce the cost of investing in homes or jobs by the private sector.

Public investments and affordable housing strategy in the past resulted in a sidewalk being repaired here, a street being fixed there, and housing scattered over a wide area. Our revised strategy was to cluster private and public investments to show dramatic turnaround in an entire neighborhood and encourage a ripple effect from a revitalized core.

Building Better Neighborhoods

Our first step in Indianapolis was to reinvest the savings from competition in Building Better Neighborhoods, an infrastructure improvement program which predominantly targeted seven deteriorating inner-city neighborhoods. Over the next five years Indianapolis invested more than $750 million repairing worn-down infrastructure. We rebuilt curbs and sidewalks, repaired sewer lines, resurfaced streets, and improved parks all over town. We rehabilitated public housing and upgraded fire and police stations. As a result of Building Better Neighborhoods, dilapidated streets are smooth again, and new parks have been built where there once was debris.

These investments were vital to restoring the economies of these neighborhoods, but they were perhaps more important in reviving their spirit. An excellent article by *Indianapolis News* reporters Judith Cebula, Shari Finnell, and Nelson Price on Christmas Day in 1993, headlined, "Miracles on 34th Street," described the impact of our infrastructure program:

> From her living room window, Ida Jordan gets a good view of 34th Street in the near north side neighborhood she has called home for 38 years. Just outside her house she sees her miracle—a new sidewalk spreading like a carpet in front of her lawn. "It's the first new thing this neighborhood has seen in years," said Jordan, 79.
>
> That concrete is a simple symbol of change in a neighborhood beginning to heal after years of decay and disruption. "When I moved here it was nice. Lots of good people taking care of the place," she said. "During the '60s and '70s it was very bad. There was a lot of gang war, young people and gunfire."

But during the past decade, the 1000 block of West 34th Street has quieted. Gangs have moved out, Jordan said, as homeowners have reclaimed the neighborhood. "The people that live in this neighborhood are quiet," Jordan said. "No one ever bothers nobody. No one causes a disturbance."

And when she looks outside her window now, Jordan sees a symbol of change—new sidewalks laid this month. "It's a miracle," she says.

It is just a sidewalk to us, but to people in troubled neighborhoods it is an important symbol that their city and government care about them. This was particularly important because we believed success depended on reversing the pity strategy and enlisting the participation of the neighborhoods themselves in rebuilding their economies.

One critical change in our approach to infrastructure investments cut right to the heart of the big-government responses that infused city governments across the country. Having decided to spend tax dollars to help a deteriorating neighborhood, the traditional approach was for well-educated, highly trained city planners and civil engineers to evaluate the needs of the neighborhood and determine for the residents what was in their best interest. But because value is whatever the customer wants, we were not producing maximum value with our institutionalized attitude of patronizing residents of poor neighborhoods.

This hit home when I visited a neighborhood meeting on the city's east side shortly after my election. City planners had decided that one of the anchors of the neighborhood, Ellenberger Park, needed more parking spaces, at a projected cost of $700,000.

When the neighborhood learned of the city's plans—after $100,000 had already been spent on new asphalt—residents erupted. Not only did they have better uses for the money, but additional parking spaces at Ellenberger were precisely what they did not want. Most of the people who drove to the park, neighborhood leaders said, were from outside the area and had come to cause trouble. We listened, and spent $35,000 tearing out the asphalt and replanting grass.

Incidents like this one had

The collision course between Republicans and Democrats continued at the local level until, in the early 1990s, a new group of mayors emerged.

been occurring for years. Across town from Ellenberger, in Haughville, the Reverend Arthur Johnson was a committed, energetic force for good. On one of my annual visits to his church as prosecutor, he took me to the street separating his new church from its parking lot and complained that the street flooded whenever it rained. Reverend Johnson had accomplished his own miracle by raising the money to build a new church, yet the city would not fix the curb drainage which caused the street to turn into a small stream on rainy days. This tiny, easily fixable problem screamed to the congregation that the city did not care.

It should have come as no surprise, therefore, when our efforts to rebuild these neighborhoods ran into twenty years of accumulated skepticism from residents. Indianapolis had long operated a "sweat equity" housing program, which offered abandoned homes for $1—with the condition that the purchaser fix it up and live in it. I decided to try a similar approach with our infrastructure dollars, and create a sweat equity program offering top priority to neighborhoods where residents would agree to organize paint-up and fix-up efforts for their blocks and parks. I took the idea to a neighborhood meeting at the Christamore House, a social service center in the heart of Haughville.

From the audience, a man stood up and stated flatly that the city had ignored Haughville for too long. He had no confidence we would live up to our end of the bargain, and he refused to enlist the help of his neighbors until we proved we were serious. "Face up to your responsibilities," he said, "and then we will respond." In my heart, I knew he had a point. That man, named Olgin Williams, would soon become one of the most effective neighborhood leaders in the city.

Not long after my failed attempt to leverage our infrastructure investments into neighborhood activism, I visited Fountain Square, a neighborhood on the city's southeast side. I was there to announce several infrastructure investments through the Building Better Neighborhoods program and had every reason to expect a warm welcome. Instead, I was greeted by children picketing the press conference and carrying signs demanding a new neighborhood park. The children complained they had no place to play; their mothers told me of syringes lying in plain sight on the streets and open drainage holes as big as craters. I turned to Estelle Perkins, one of the leaders of the demonstration, and asked what she wanted first. More police and a new playground, she said without missing a beat. She proceeded to tell me precisely where the playground could go. In retrospect, I would like to say that my earlier experience with Olgin Williams convinced me that I needed a quick victory to show neighborhood leaders we were serious about the area; but in reality I simply spoke without thinking. I told Estelle the city would have a park and playground equipment on the spot she identified within ninety days. When Estelle and I cut the ribbon on that park ninety days later, everyone was amazed—including me. Gradually, we began to build trust between City Hall and the neighborhoods.

Enhancing Grassroots Leadership

As Haughville, Fountain Square, and a dozen other neighborhoods showed us, even City Hall was too far away to understand a neighborhood, much less design a strategy to revitalize it. We needed to work with the indigenous leadership of these neighborhoods first to identify the real problems, and then to implement solutions that would be more than just quick fixes.

In our desire to push government down to the neighborhood level, we encouraged residents and community organizations to tell us how services should be delivered in their neighborhood. Just as reformers in Washington, DC, would soon embark on efforts to devolve authority to states and cities, we were trying to devolve power from City Hall to dozens of neighborhood-level organizations. Robert Woodson brought me into contact with some of the remarkable grassroots leaders around the country identified by Jack Kemp when he served as secretary of the Department of Housing and Urban Development. I was determined to allow our neighborhood leaders to have the same opportunities.

Shortly after returning from a meeting with Woodson, I met a public housing resident named Saundra Bailey, who ran a cleaning service that employed several of her fellow residents of public housing. She offered a few positive comments about conditions in the neighborhood, but complained about the absence of a variety store. Using my best empowerment language, I suggested she consider opening her own. Astonished, she quickly brought me back to earth by asking what I thought she knew about running a variety store.

To make neighborhood empowerment work, we needed more Violets and Olgins, and we needed to give new skills to Saundra and leaders like her.

We started by creating the Neighborhood Resource Center. The center, operated by a board of community representatives, serves as a school to promote grassroots activism and teach the skills necessary to succeed in redevelopment activities. Since 1994 the Neighborhood Resource Center has helped create eighty new neighborhood and homeowner associations. Graduates of the program have made an immediate impact on their respective neighborhoods—from playing an active role in the financial management of their communities to winning zoning cases.

Some neighborhood associations were active enough to warrant full-time staff. In response, we created the Neighborhood Empowerment Initiative, funded with grants from the Annie Casey Foundation, the Lilly Endowment, and the Ford Foundation. The foundations provided funding so that an advocate could be located in each of our targeted neighborhoods. We did not want to use city funds for the positions in fear that this would co-opt the grassroots activism we were trying to create. Early in my first term, I toured Baltimore's Sandtown, an urban area adopted as a joint effort between the late urban developer James Rouse and the city of Baltimore. My tour guide, recommended to me by Mayor Kurt Schmoke, proudly told me he was a neighborhood leader who worked closely with the city, but that he was paid by and represented the neighbors.

Our advocates assisted with economic development, published newsletters, and helped to formulate goals, needs, and strategies. One of these representatives once asked me how I would know when he succeeded. I answered, only half-jokingly, "When your residents become interested enough to march on City Hall to demand better services, I'll know that we've made it."

Next, we attempted to invest city and federal dollars in a way that expanded the number of persons who had a stake in the success of the area. Since home ownership causes people to care about their property and its value, we wanted to strengthen the community development corporations that involve neighbors in the planning and production of urban housing. The Indianapolis Neighborhood Housing Partnership Corporation, a not-for-profit organization that specialized in arranging affordable home financing, launched a five-year effort to build homes and, more significantly, to build neighborhood capacity. Over $100 million in investment was raised in conjunction with local community development corporations and the Local Initiatives Support Corporation, a national leader in affordable housing strategies

This effort produced remarkable results. In the older, more difficult areas more than 3,700 houses have been rehabilitated and hundreds more new houses built in the past four years, tripling previous efforts. All this comes at a time when the Department of Metropolitan Development—the department that deals with housing—has been downsized by a third since 1992. Operating dollars were converted, in effect, into infrastructure dollars.

Looking back, we reached a turning point on the day that Carolyn Hook, a mother from Fountain Square, visited my office with a group of fellow residents. Armed with maps, photographs, and court records, these women presented me with a list of abandoned buildings being used by crack dealers, street corners being used by prostitutes, and a variety of other neighborhood nuisances. In other words, the neighborhood began to have confidence that the city would respond, and produced valuable information to help us make the neighborhood safer.

Interestingly, Carolyn also complained about zoning, and how the city enforced health and safety regulations in Fountain Square. In response, we created neighborhood-based code compliance committees to identify nuisances that should be targeted by city health and building code enforcement officials.

Carolyn and her neighbors then went back to Fountain Square and took up the fight with us. She organized antidrug marches in high-crime areas, and staged Friday night picket lines around crack houses. In the six months following our meeting, violent crime in Fountain Square plummeted and twenty-five drug houses were put out of business.

In *The Death and Life of Great American Cities* (1961), Jane Jacob described the social fabric of neighborhoods that maintains order:

> The first thing to understand is that the public peace—the sidewalk and street peace—of cities is not kept primarily by the police, necessary as police are. It is kept primarily by an intricate, almost unconscious, network of voluntary controls and standards among the people themselves, and enforced by the people themselves. In some city areas—older public housing projects and streets with very high population turnover are often conspicuous examples—the keeping of public sidewalk law and order is left almost entirely to the police and special guards. Such places are jungles. No amount of police can enforce civilization where the normal, casual enforcement of it has broken down.

Fountain Square became a better place to live for one reason—because the neighborhood flexed its muscles and decided that it would not abide the presence of drug dealers. Once again, our own Violet Gwin said it well:

> I tell people that your neighborhood is what you will tolerate. If you tolerate drugs, crime, prostitution, welfare—whatever—that's what your neighborhood will be like. If you will not tolerate these things and you get

active yourself, you can eradicate a lot of them before they come to you, or if you've got them already, you can get rid of them. If you will tolerate abandoned cars, if you will tolerate drug houses, if you will tolerate all these things in a community then that's what your community is going to be like. It's not going to be long before your community is considered a ghetto.

The twenty-three acre site on the edge of the park had been a "Whites Only" amusement park—it was both a symbol of the worst racist attitudes of an earlier time and of the current real-life dangers facing this now African American neighborhood.

The importance of neighborhood participation is one reason why community policing is such a critical step for police departments across the country. But neighborhood leadership is vital to more than just fighting crime. Every aspect of improving community life depends upon a strong community fabric.

Curing Disinvestment

In Fountain Square, we put in a new police substation and stepped up bicycle and foot patrols. We repaired the fountain of Fountain Square—an important symbol for the neighborhood. The Southeast Neighborhood Development Corporation (SEND), one of 14 community development corporations in the city, did an outstanding job representing Fountain Square. As SEND and its skillful director Bill Taft put together coalitions, raised money, and developed property, it generated enthusiasm, support, and success. Over a two-year period we spent more than $5.5 million on housing and infrastructure in Fountain Square to help cure the years of neglect.

I've already told you about the park we built in ninety days. We also assisted SEND in renovating over a hundred houses. Representatives of the city communicated with every small business in the area, encouraging them to expand. City attention created confidence in Fountain Square's future, which created hundreds of jobs and millions in investments. A vacant, six-story building faced the square, a vivid example of decay. On the other side an old theater stood vacant, its marquee dark. Taft convinced the public library to occupy the first floor of the six-story building, and it provided enough rent to allow them to develop the remainder as apartments for seniors. A local couple purchased the theater, opened a diner on the first floor, and renovated the facade.

The redevelopment of Fountain Square produced the hoped for ripple effect. Tax credits and loans facilitated a $4.9 million project to build twenty-two new townhouses and renovate five doubles. Creative financial partnerships restored homes at reduced rates, allowing more renters to purchase homes at affordable prices. Instead of fleeing, middle-class residents stayed or moved in and helped renovate. Jobs and commercial investment created millions in new investments. The partnership that took off the day the mothers confronted me about the park has borne fruit for the neighborhood and made Fountain Square a national example of what can be done by people who care.

Mark Stokes, the leader of a community development corporation in Haughville, was another expert in leveraging government spending into private investment. One day Mark walked me through an abandoned rail switchyard, pointing out opportunities for bringing jobs into the neighborhood. The site had rail access, good roads, a central location, and a large labor supply nearby. But the land was burdened with old buildings, a bad reputation, and the typical fright that environmental regulators unfortunately create, scaring away investors for fear of untold environmental liabilities.

The city acquired the land for $600,000 and spent $270,000 on environmental remediation. The city encouraged investment by providing much more attractive incentives for businesses willing to locate in high-unemployment areas, such as the near west side. The public hospital built a $1.5 million health center, bringing new services and outreach programs to the area.

Today, the near westside area that includes Haughville is on the way back. Barely two years later, after my walk with Mark Stokes, four companies occupy this once condemned eyesore. EHOB, a high-quality medical device manufacturer, has taken 7.5 acres and invested $2.5 million on a 60,000-square foot facility. Dickey & Sons, a machine tool company, invested $1.7 million in another 60,000-square foot facility. Sims Cabinet Company, an existing neighboring business, encouraged by the new investors, acquired 2.5 acres for future expansion. The remaining 3.1 acres will be developed by Carter Plastic, a minority-owned business that will invest approximately $4 million and create seventy new jobs. A little city intervention turned this once abandoned commercial site into an asset, producing jobs and paying taxes. Willing neighbors interested in jobs eagerly greeted the companies.

Rediscovering Natural Assets

By 1992 most of Indianapolis's two hundred parks were over thirty years old and had never been renovated. Smaller neighborhood parks generally had cracked tennis courts, unsafe playground equipment, and basketball courts without rims. Drug dealers staked out their turf in some of the city's more neglected parks. The combination of disrepair and criminal occupation turned what should have been assets into liabilities. With philanthropic help from Lilly Endowment we set out to remake the city's park system, using its physical assets to stabilize surrounding areas.

An amenity like a park can do wonders for a neighborhood. We set aside $41.2 million in Building Better Neighborhoods funds to rescue decayed parks and use them to increase property values. More than eighty projects to improve Indianapolis parks were launched. Our investments even inspired residents in some neighborhoods to raise their own money for additional programs and capital, with the hope that increased activity would drive out drug dealers and persons who committed undesirable acts.

We selected the area represented by the United Northwest Area neighborhood association (UNWA) as one of the toughest communities where we hoped to make a difference. UNWA was an umbrella group over many different neighborhood associations, some strong and some not. Its Community Development Corporation was less experienced than those in Fountain Square and Haughville, and its decay spread over a larger area. But 976 acres of city-owned park property sprawled along its western perimeter. We reasoned that since suburban developers created much lesser amenities to market their home and business sites, this wonderful area could be reclaimed and revitalized, and could serve to stabilize the area. I undertook an effort to transform the beautiful but unsafe property into a safe, busy regional park on the White River. It now includes pedestrian and bike paths, boat rentals, basketball courts, a golf academy, and three renovated and privately managed golf courses. A new community center, pool, and gym reached out to the young adults.

In addition to the daily positive interaction that takes place in city parks, well-kept public spaces have a positive spill over effect on their neighborhoods. We viewed Riverside Park as a tool in upgrading the neighborhood housing stock. The first few streets adjoining the park contain nice homes, some needing repair, but generally well kept. As one moves west to east away from the park the number of crack houses, vacant lots, and abandoned industrial sites increases. A door-to-door survey conducted by UNWA identified houses that needed repair. Federal housing funds, granted by the city to UNWA, helped reduce the cost of remodeling.

We still wanted to get more people living near the park, thus filling intimidating, vacant spaces with lively urban neighborhoods. One twenty-three–acre site on the edge of the park had been a "Whites Only" amusement park in the past. It was both a symbol of the worst racist attitudes of an earlier time and of the current real-life dangers facing this now African American neighborhood. I asked Methodist Hospital, a very large private institution located two miles away, and the Citizens Gas Company to help the community. Methodist and Citizens teamed with the UNWA community development corporation, providing it with technical assistance and money for housing.

We are proud of what we did in the city's troubled neighborhoods, and we see Indianapolis as a national model—a city that really works for the twenty-first century.

The community responded enthusiastically. But then we ran into trouble that illustrated the depth of the gulf between suburban and urban neighborhoods. The leadership of the suburban Nora Community Council rose up to wage war on the neighborhood and me. They insisted that the housing would reduce their access to the river. They raised health concerns. They worked with an environmental group that sued to stop the project. But the Riverside community, despite its evident problems, had two confident, well-organized community activists in the persons of Lillian Davis and Mary Artist.

They rallied the neighborhood, negotiated land use, fought to keep the city interested in the neighborhood, and won. An area once so unsafe that the nearest neighbor, a Naval Armory, surrounded itself with barbed wire and encouraged Marines to jog in pairs, is experiencing the development of 140 condominiums valued at $80,000 to $150,000 per unit.

Touching All the Bases

We are proud of what we did in the city's troubled neighborhoods, and we see Indianapolis as a national model of what really works for the twenty-first century. But we made plenty of mistakes, and there are plenty of things we will do differently in the future.

Ironically, one of our mistakes was not following our own market-driven philosophy on occasion and relying too heavily on government action to revive a neighborhood.

For example, two neighborhoods, the Meadows and Fall Creek, failed early to meet their enormous potential. Although the Meadows, located in northeastern Indianapolis, had once been a stable, working-class neighborhood, it was in trouble when I took office.

Local firebrand Violet Gwin demanded help. Writing, button-holing my predecessor and me at meetings, alternately yelling at and hugging me, she pleaded for assistance. I decided it was time to get city government involved in the Meadows. We spent $3 million improving the infrastructure. The focus of our effort was an abandoned strip mall. Here the city bought land for a new $10 million, 72,400-square foot grocery store. It was the first new retail outlet in the neighborhood in forty years.

Neighbors rejoiced. New fast-food operations and several small retailers, including drug, fast food, video, and other stores, moved into the area. The future looked bright. But the expected renaissance did not occur. What did we learn? That city efforts can make it easier for investment to occur but cannot create a market. Residents still did not feel safe in the Meadows. The fragile economy of a transitional neighborhood needs all the pieces to be in place: investment, committed neighborhoods, public safety, and schools. Missing even one piece—for example, lacking public safety—can jeopardize a rebirth.

We have not given up on the Meadows. We added more police patrols, put in new street lights, and helped work out a change in ownership for a large apartment complex, resulting in the demolition of many vacant units.

Similar problems occurred when we tried to redevelop Fall Creek proper, once a nice middle-class area. Steve Scott, a neighborhood resident and developer, saw vast potential here. Situated on the banks of a small creek, the neighborhood had a nice greenway. Steve saw the creek as an amenity that would help him sell market-rate homes starting at $85,000, but he needed help from the city to secure ownership of land, since one or two recalcitrant slumlords can retard a redevelopment effort.

In response, the city acquired land, demolished twenty old structures, and agreed to build sidewalks, clean up along the banks, and erect a beautiful promenade. After six months, I visited Steve on the site. But little had actually been built other than curbs. City officials, rightly worried about money, had refused to start the cleanup and building of the abutting promenades.

I asked city planners to get to work on the project. I urged them to evict residents illegally occupying houses in the area and to finish the roads and work on the creek bank. They did. But Fall Creek was not the success I had anticipated. Only seven of the fifty-two lots in Fall Creek had sold within ninety days. What was wrong? Poor schools. Families who could afford the houses did not want their children to attend the nearby public schools, and were not quite in the income range where private schools were an option. All the factors had to be in place for the rebirth. We encouraged a local business to provide money for private school scholarships to new purchasers with children, and included this fact in our marketing. Several homes sold immediately.

Neighborhood redevelopment is a perilous adventure. Everything must line up to turn neighborhoods around. Some government help—not too much—and the right local leaders can still improve the toughest areas. At almost every stage the tension between too much and too little government exists.

Public dollars must help reduce the cost of land acquisition and environmental compliance. But government dollars cannot make a retail project successful without customers who are willing to pay for the product. Low-interest loans and small grants can help people buy homes, but if the neighborhood is unsafe and the schools poor the homes will go unsold.

Many of our neighborhoods are now on the way back, but not without fits, and starts, and mistakes made by all of us.

Chapter Eleven

Rebuilding Civil Society

There was a time when most children came from strong, two-parent families who taught a value system and belief in God. They were surrounded by authority figures like ministers and neighbors; and in the background the sanctioning role of the law inspired good behavior when temptation beckoned.

Today, fewer children grow up in stable homes with parents who care for and discipline them. These children are left exposed to the negative undercurrents of American culture. No one believes that listening to a Snoop Doggy Dogg album causes a child to join a gang or commit a crime, but each year the currents beat at children whose moral compasses are less and less sure.

With their bearings weakened, many of these children soon learn another lesson: that the chance of being convicted of a crime as a juvenile is slim, and the danger of serving a meaningful sentence is virtually nonexistent. Take auto theft as an example.

From the judge's viewpoint, a seventeen-year-old car thief who comes to court neatly dressed and acting reasonably remorseful is someone to whom a break can be given—one less inmate for an overcrowded prison system. But stealing cars is one of the entry-level jobs of crime, and when the judge dismisses the case, another youth walks away with the message that anything goes.

Public schools once served an important role in communicating values, but today many educators believe that morality is outside the bounds of the classroom. They are more concerned with building self-esteem than building character. Advocates of condom distribution in the schools send the message that children are helpless victims of their hormones, not moral agents-in-training with the ability to choose good behavior. "They're going to do it anyway" replaces "Just say no" as the mantra of the day.

Moral encouragement isn't the only thing missing from the classroom—few school systems even enforce truancy rigorously anymore, sending the message that education itself is another value that society does not take seriously. In many schools, teachers and counselors quietly encourage at-risk kids to drop out, breathing a sigh of relief when they are gone. And the ties of society weaken further.

No longer backed up by the law or the schools, a neighbor who once would have felt at ease disciplining a neighborhood child now passes by quietly, avoiding eye contact and hoping not to become a victim of juvenile violence. An Indianapolis minister who tried to rid his neighborhood of a crack house was assaulted by teenage boys who put a gun to his head and promised to kill him if he interfered again.

I do not know how to solve this problem. I do know that fixing our juvenile justice system and our schools is the easy part. Reviving civility and community is hard, and without religion it is impossible.

Government programs are not the answer. No ordinance, no regulation, no social service can cause people to behave morally. The only way to mend the holes in our social fabric is through the traditional institutions that have always communicated values: families, religious institutions, schools, neighborhood associations, and community groups.

Encouraging Families

The family is the fundamental unit of every successful society. But for the past thirty-plus years, government has consistently undermined this source of public virtue. Government has taken money away from families through ever-increasing taxes and then perversely used some of the revenues on programs that actively discourage poor Americans from forming families—rewarding teenage and out-of-wedlock pregnancies, discouraging fathers from living with the mothers of their children, and failing to hold those fathers accountable for even the smallest amount of support.

The negative effects of single, teenage parenthood on our society are difficult to overstate. David Blankenhorn, in his book *Fatherless America* (1995), offers a chilling indictment of the state of the American family:

> The most urgent domestic challenge facing the United States at the close of the 20th century is the re-creation of fatherhood as a vital social role for men. For unless we reverse the trend of fatherlessness, no other set of accomplishments—not economic growth, or prison construction, or welfare reform, or better schools—will succeed in arresting the decline of child welfare and the spread of male violence.

Nothing that government can do will restore civility to our neighborhoods in the face of rising illegitimacy. But government can battle this trend by promoting abstinence among teenage men and women, by ensuring that irresponsible fatherhood yields consequences, and by supporting vulnerable families.

In 1992 federal, state, and local governments spent $305 billion on welfare programs—more than eight times as much as in 1965. Over the past thirty years more than $5 trillion has been spent on welfare. Yet this enormous expenditure represents a fraction of the true cost of America's welfare policies. The real tragedy of the program lies in the perverse incentives built into the welfare system and the human dysfunction they have fostered.

From 1960 to 1990 the percentage of babies born outside of marriage in the United States increased from 5.3 percent to 29.5 percent, and today the United States has the highest proportion of fatherless households in the world. The numbers in Indianapolis are even more discouraging. Indianapolis suffers an out-of-wedlock birth rate of 40 percent—well above the national average. Fully a quarter of our children live in a home with no father. And the numbers for teens, whose birth rates increased by more than 40 percent over the past decade, are even more astounding. Eighty-nine percent of Indianapolis teenagers who gave birth last year were not married.

The negative consequences of out-of-wedlock childbearing reach far beyond single mothers and their children. One obvious consequence is the proliferation of juvenile crime. According to social researchers William Galston and Elaine Kamarck, the relationship between crime and family structure is so strong "that controlling for family configuration erases the relationship between race and crime and between low income and crime."

This observation is confirmed by experience, both in Indianapolis and across the country. Nationally, 75 percent of adolescent murderers, nearly 66 percent of all rapists, and 70 percent of

all prison and reform-school inmates grew up without fathers in
their homes. In Indianapolis, while the overall crime rate has
remained stable for the past ten years, the juvenile crime rate has
increased nearly fivefold. Juvenile Court Judge James Payne estimates that 75 percent of the delinquents he adjudicates come from
homes without fathers.

It doesn't stop with crime.
Children without fathers face a
wide range of serious problems,
including twice the risk of
dropping out of high school and five times the risk of being poor.

Reviving civility and community is hard, and without religion it is impossible.

Government cannot create two-parent families, but there are
things that government can do—and stop doing—that would discourage teen pregnancy and single parenthood and promote
responsible fatherhood. In September of 1995 the City of Indianapolis launched a series of initiatives to confront directly and
comprehensively the problem of family breakdown. The Rebuilding Families program, established with the support and encouragement of Indianapolis's leading religious, nonprofit, and social
service organizations, employs a wide range of strategies to reduce
single parenthood and improve the support and economic opportunities available to vulnerable families.

Standards and Stigma

Sadly, most public officials accept teenage pregnancy. Too often
their efforts to help teen mothers end up encouraging the very
behavior that is at the root of the problem. Schools committed to
mainstreaming pregnant teens, for example, convey the message
that public institutions will go to great lengths to ensure that those
who engage in irresponsible behavior will suffer no consequences
for their actions. This tacit acceptance, coupled with the permissive attitude toward premarital sex that pervades popular culture,

helps create an environment in which teens, and even their adult role models, ridicule the very notion of abstinence.

The Rebuilding Families initiative aims to combat this "normalization" of teen pregnancy and to reinforce the understanding that teen pregnancy is wrong. But the prevalence of cultural messages condoning premarital sex and strong peer group acceptance of teen parenthood convinced me that no single response would be sufficient to address the problem. We therefore undertook a number of activities designed to shift the balance of the messages our young people receive in favor of abstinence and responsible behavior.

Before deciding on program content, we sought first-hand information, especially the views of teenagers themselves. As we visited high schools and middle schools and talked to students in focus groups about these issues, even preteens said they felt overwhelming pressure from their peers to engage in sexual conduct.

This discovery led us to champion the successful peer mentoring program called A Promise to Keep. The program, developed through a collaboration among St. Vincent Hospital, St. Francis Hospital, and the Indianapolis Archdiocese's Office of Catholic Education, uses the power of peer pressure to promote abstinence among teenage youth. It operates under the principle that adults other than parents are too far removed from teen culture to compel young people to choose to be chaste. Founder Eve Jackson, a home economics teacher at Hamilton Southeastern High School in Indianapolis, created the program in response to frequent questions she received from students confused about sex.

Older, self-confident teens serve as powerful advocates for chastity, and compete with teen idols in the media who endorse premarital sex. Similar programs in other cities have helped reduce teen pregnancy by as much as 30 percent. These successes and early positive reviews inspired Indianapolis's Methodist Hospital to implement a secular version of A Promise to Keep in Indianapolis Public Schools, which have an intolerably high teenage pregnancy rate. The program is so popular that more than two hundred students recently competed for the honor of serving as mentors.

We also targeted school policies that failed to discourage teen parenthood. Most public schools, for instance, adopt standards for student athletes, requiring them to refrain from drinking or using drugs and to maintain a certain grade point average and attendance record. Conspicuously absent from these requirements is not fathering a child. We called upon school officials to send a clear message that adult behavior nets adult responsibility by precluding teen fathers from participating in school athletic activities. We wanted to change the conversation in school locker rooms from sexual boasting to abstinence.

But virtually all school officials believe that they should not set standards about sexual behavior, and thus far remain firmly against the policy. My trips to schools after this skirmish demonstrated that we had at least fueled a conversation on the topic—a minor victory—but also indicated the depth of the problem. The daughter of a prominent business leader, attending one of the city's top private schools, asked me during one visit if I was really advocating that teen dads not be allowed to play sports, and if so what right did I have to set standards of conduct for students.

We have also attempted to spark parental pressure and teacher concern by releasing the number of births by school from information compiled from birth records. Although school administrators have yet to budge, we hope that focusing attention on the comparative data will eventually create a sense of urgency and outrage.

Rebuilding Families attempts to balance the flood of messages in popular culture that implicitly endorse premarital sexual activity. We are not interested in providing teens with tips on how to have "safe" sex. Unlike a public service announcement I watched recently on network television, which featured a popular celebrity cautioning against casual sex because of the risk of venereal disease, we emphasize right and wrong. In the schools and in public service announcements with local celebrities, we emphasize abstinence and the wrongful nature of teen parenting.

There is nothing inconsistent with stigmatizing irresponsible behavior while maintaining a firm commitment to helping young women who need support. Research indicates that 31 percent of young women who give birth under the age of seventeen have an additional child within two years. We can reduce the teen pregnancy rate dramatically by aiming prevention efforts at these at-risk young women and providing them with the support and incentives necessary to keep them in school, while remaining steadfastly and vocally committed to the proposition that their behavior is wrong.

Accountability and Consequences

Single motherhood is a challenge even when fathers are responsible and live up to their child-support obligations. Without support payments it is virtually impossible for low-income mothers to raise their children without assistance—usually from taxpayers. One of the few services government can provide that private groups cannot is child-support enforcement. Unfortunately, in most states there are few consequences for a young father who chooses to ignore his child.

Holding fathers accountable for their children improves the financial situation of mothers and children, encourages fathers to be active in their children's lives, and may even reduce out-of-wedlock births. Research indicates that government can make a significant, positive impact on the behavior of would-be fathers simply by ensuring that they face the consequences of their actions. Unfortunately, although federal law requires mothers to cooperate in establishing paternity as a condition of receiving welfare benefits, the degree of enforcement varies widely. Georgia led all states in 1995 with a paternity establishment rate of 91 percent; in contrast, Oklahoma registered a scant 16 percent the same year (up from 3 percent in 1992). Nationally, the average paternity establishment rate in 1995 was 50 percent. Vigorous action while the mother is still in the hospital can improve these results. In Ohio, for example, a policy that pays hospitals a mere $5.20 for each information packet delivered to a birthing mother on the importance of establishing paternity has increased the paternity establishment rate by nearly 30 percent.

Establishing paternity alone will accomplish little, however, as long as a young man can easily escape any real consequence for his action. Delinquent fathers ordered to court on contempt charges often claim inability to pay. Because of limited jail space, judges tend to order those fathers to find work, only to have them return a month later with the same story and the same result.

In many parts of the country, including Indianapolis, prosecutors have the duty of collecting child support. In my twelve years as prosecutor I made child-support enforcement a priority, increasing collections from $900,000 a year to $36 million in twelve years and improving paternity establishment substantially. I was flattered some years ago when an appreciative welfare recipient confided that she used my name as a verb to threaten a would-be father—as a sort of action she would take against him if he refused to pay support. Stories like these led me to consider enforcement not just as a revenue mechanism but as a way to alter conduct.

Toward that end, we created the Job or Jail program, which gave judges an alternative that would enable unemployed parents to fulfill their financial obligations by connecting them with private sector employers. Judges refer unemployed fathers to a job-readiness program run by the Indianapolis Private Industry Council. The court orders those who do not take advantage of this opportunity into community service. They work for city departments picking up trash, cleaning garages, and maintaining parks. In other words, fathers who *will not* work to support their children *will* work to support the taxpayers who are supporting their children. Once a parent secures employment, the court suspends the sentence of community work. Fathers who refuse to get a job or enroll in job readiness training under this arrangement are jailed, then made to do community work as trustees of the jail.

Even when fathers do pay child support, those payments do little to help if the mother is on AFDC. Mothers on welfare see little benefit, because almost all of the support a father pays actually goes to the welfare department to repay it for AFDC payments previously made to the mother. The proper destination for child-support payments is the mother herself, not the government. Making this simple and obvious change to the child-support system could have a dramatic positive impact on the ability of welfare mothers to achieve self-sufficiency and would further encourage responsibility on the part of fathers.

Government can also play a constructive role simply by enforcing previously ignored existing laws. National estimates suggest that 30 percent to 50 percent of men who impregnate teenage girls are more than five years older than the young mothers (on average, the fathers are 3.5 years older). Similarly, 74 percent of women who have intercourse before age fourteen and 60 percent of those who have sex before age fifteen report having had sex involuntarily. Indianapolis prosecutor Scott Newman and a few other district attorneys around the country recently began to revive long-unused statutory rape laws and aggressively prosecute violators. In 1996 Newman convicted five men, with fifteen cases pending. All of the girls involved were fifteen or younger. We are hopeful that consistent prosecution under statutory rape laws will change the attitudes of young men and protect the girls who might otherwise be affected.

Again, our insistence on parental responsibility does not preclude us from supporting these young men. On the contrary, programs like the Father Resource Center teach these fathers parenting and job skills and connect them with work.

> **Communities of faith can do more to help strengthen families than any government agency can hope to accomplish.**

This combination of assistance and enforcement helps fathers to provide for their children while demonstrating in no uncertain terms a commitment to holding them accountable.

Faith and Families

Religious institutions are in an ideal position to intervene in the lives of distressed families. Communities of faith can do more to help strengthen families than any government agency can hope to accomplish. A little over a year ago, we asked religious leaders to advise city officials and to elevate the discussion about illegitimacy, marriage, and teenage pregnancy. The clergy not only preached on the subject, they helped to develop the Faith and Families program of Indiana.

Inspired by the Faith and Families program in Mississippi, leaders from the religious community came together to develop a model that links vulnerable families with congregations in order to help single parents achieve and maintain employment. For teenage parents, the program offers the support they need to complete school and find employment, and encourages them to delay having additional children until they are married and self-sufficient. The program also links congregations with each other, resulting in a number of effective urban–suburban partnerships.

Faith and Families operates without any public support. It is funded entirely by grants from private charitable organizations. Since the program's inception a year ago, twenty-three congregations in Indianapolis have assisted nearly fifty families. One person helped by the program is Tanya, a nineteen-year-old single mother of two young daughters. Tanya grew up in a home headed by an alcoholic mother, lived in a group home for some time, and was eventually emancipated by juvenile court. Tanya was fortunate to escape an abusive relationship with the father of her second child, and she received some child support and social security for her older daughter. But by the time Tanya entered the Faith and Families program, she was homeless and living in a church-based shelter for destitute families.

The program linked Tanya with members of St. Luke's United Methodist Church, who helped her find a job and her own apartment. Today, Tanya is a certified nursing assistant and has plans to attend college at night. She also worships at St. Luke's and attends a service for young singles there. She believes the congregation's support gave her and her children a new lease on life.

Faith and Families director Richard Wiehe says that the program has also affected the lives of church members, who are enriched by their efforts to improve the lives of the less fortunate. Such efforts, which lie at the heart of the ethic that pervades American communities of faith, provide clear evidence of the vital role religion can and must play in restoring civil society.

Supporting Mediating Institutions

When we began to improve some of Indianapolis's run-down neighborhoods, we looked to religious and neighborhood groups for help.

While we met many wonderful leaders, we also made an alarming discovery: these institutions were not what they used to be.

When government attempted to acquire a monopoly on the provision of good deeds in inner cities, it both created and filled a void. Instead of communities, congregations, or kin bonding to provide care for the needy and enforce responsibility, the government wrote checks—seemingly limitless checks—transforming charity into an intergenerational entitlement. The network of charitable organizations that had protected the weak in former times had withered away.

Nobody recognizes the magnitude of our loss for further generations better than *Book of Virtues* (1993) author William Bennett. Writing in the March 1995 issue of *Commentary* magazine, Bennett observed:

> The greatest long-term threat to the well-being of our children is the enfeebled condition—in some sectors of our society, the near collapse—of our character-forming institutions. In a free society, families, schools, and churches have primary responsibility for shaping the moral sensibilities of the young. The influence of these institutions is determinative; when they no longer provide moral instruction or lose their moral authority, there is very little that auxiliaries—particularly the federal government—can do.

Supporting Religion

Theodore Roosevelt's vision of the social role of our churches is as relevant today as it was when he spoke in a church in 1902:

> The forces for evil, as our cities grow, become more concentrated, more menacing to the community, and if

the community is to go forward and not backward they must be met and overcome by forces for good that have grown in corresponding degree. More and more in the future our churches must take the lead in shaping those forces for good.

Sadly, many of those in government today seem to have lost Roosevelt's vision. Elected leaders often shy away from religion because of its political volatility and because they do not want to interfere in personal decisions. Far worse, in some cases government is openly antagonistic to religion, creating unnecessary obstacles to religious groups that strive to help those in need.

Only hardened skeptics have trouble accepting the idea that widespread belief in a Supreme Being improves the strength and health of our communities. Those who possess strongly held religious convictions conduct themselves with civility because of their beliefs, not simply because a police officer is on the opposite corner. A recent Heritage Foundation report summarized some fascinating research that showed the connection between religion and healthy families and communities. Among other things, it reported that consistent religious practice brings marital stability; helps poor persons move out of poverty, especially young inner-city residents; contributes substantially to the formation of personal character and sound moral judgment; inoculates individuals against a host of social problems, including suicide, drug abuse, crime, and out-of-wedlock births; and encourages beneficial effects on mental health and self-esteem.

Religion and religious institutions must play a critical role in the future of our cities, and government can assist in two ways. First, public officials should use the bully pulpit to celebrate and encourage religious commitment without favoring one tradition

over another. Second, cities can undertake initiatives with houses
of worship, as discussed below, that strengthen communities while
encouraging connections that promote religious involvement.

Churches and Parks

When inner-city youths form relationships with churches, good
things happen. In Indianapolis, crime and decay haunted many of
our two hundred parks. Near a fair number of these troubled
parks stood a church. Often the church represented the most
important mediating force in the community, yet it lacked adequate resources to program youth activities. At the same time, the
community viewed the park not as theirs, but as the city's, and
therefore did not reach out in a possessive way to protect and preserve the green and play areas.

We worked to generate interest among these churches in maintaining parks in their neighborhoods. Two church deacons, both
city employees, led the effort to create church–park relationships,
asking church-affiliated groups to help reclaim nearby parks. The
city offered small contracts to neighborhood churches and other
community groups to see if they could provide better quality services for the money.

Indianapolis now contracts with ten churches to maintain
twenty-nine city parks. Maintenance includes mowing the grass,
sweeping the walks and driveways, picking up litter, and keeping
athletic areas free of glass and debris. The parks department
continues to maintain equipment, make capital improvements,
and accept liability on park property.

These partnerships tend to drive away alcoholics and drug
addicts and allow families to return. For example, one local
church recently organized a community cleanup of a nearby park

and painted a picnic shelter once defaced with gang graffiti. The park area that residents fearfully avoided now houses a church-based summer children's camp.

Another church organized a trash patrol for children after school. Children who participate and who cannot afford the cost of park amenities (pools, for example) receive vouchers for free admission to these facilities. One participating church hired residents from its homeless shelter to cut the grass in the parks. Now local businesses pay these individuals to cut their lawns as well, and an area bank provides materials and trash can liners for all of the parks involved.

Today in Indianapolis, church leaders and neighborhood residents work together in the parks, developing a sense of ownership. They cost the city no more money than previous maintenance, take better care of the parks than the city did, and make the parks safer for general use. The city posts signs in each of these parks with the name and phone number of the involved church and the name of the pastor. Reinvigorated churches help provide services that support neighborhood-driven employment and training, social services, recreation, and housing revitalization. These partnerships not only serve to build up the economic fabric of a neighborhood, but also refocus attention on the importance of churches as sources of moral renewal.

Religion and Troubled Youth

Connecting juvenile offenders to local churches provides a stable connection for young people. More importantly, religion can help people in ways that government cannot. While the criminal justice system generally can only punish, churches can rehabilitate troubled youth by instilling in them respect, obedience, and hope.

The Indianapolis Training Center provides a remarkable example of how government can work with faith-based organizations.

The center was established by Bill Gothard, the founder of a Christian ministry that conducts teaching seminars across the country. Gothard proposed purchasing a closed hotel in the city and converting it into a training facility for young men and women, where they would participate in a biblically based program designed to instill character. We encouraged this participation, and Gothard brought in young people and their families from around the world.

Only hardened skeptics have trouble accepting the idea that widespread belief in a Supreme Being improves the strength and health of our communities.

Eventually, Gothard suggested that the center might use its strong religious and moral base to work with troubled teenage boys and girls. Today the juvenile court uses the center as an alternative to Girls' or Boys' School. The program works not only with these adolescents, but also with their families, reflecting a belief that the child who resists his parents is likely to resist the constraints of law and society as well.

The program's emphasis on values has proved an enormous success. Eighty-four percent of the juveniles assigned to the center since it opened in 1993 are offenders who have run afoul of the law multiple times. Yet in four years more than 71 percent of all juveniles sent to the center have stayed out of trouble with the law.

Now other courts refer youths to the center. A DuPage County, Illinois, judge sentenced a young woman named Minnie to the center after she had been arrested more than seventy times. When Minnie and her parents first arrived at the center, she was violently opposed to joining the program. After speaking with two young graduates of the center, however, she decided to give it a try. Over the next several months, her attitude changed dramatically, thrilling her parents and amazing the judge overseeing her case. Minnie decided to stay at the Indianapolis Training Center to complete her training to become a cosmetologist. Like the young women who convinced her to give the program a try, Minnie wants to serve other young people at juvenile detention centers in order to help them make the right choices.

These are not the kinds of stories that one generally hears about the traditional juvenile justice system, from which most kids emerge more estranged and disaffected than when they entered. While reducing crime among juveniles requires that we consistently punish criminal activity, delinquent youths need more than punishment—they need guidance. Connecting troubled youths to programs that can communicate and instill good values can be a powerful tool in reducing recidivism and stemming the tide of juvenile crime.

Faith-Based Assistance

Church-based groups are infinitely better suited than government to help vulnerable individuals. Government is typically unable to discriminate between the truly needy and those simply seeking a handout. Government programs are also prevented from instructing those on assistance about the need to exercise moral judgment in their decision making. They can offer the soup, but not the salvation.

In contrast, when church congregations help needy individuals, they do more than merely pass out checks to case numbers—they help their neighbors, thereby strengthening the bonds of community. And by making faith an integral part of that assistance, church-based efforts provide needy individuals with a source of strength and the moral impetus for personal change that government simply cannot.

Too often government usurps the role of churches in helping struggling community members. Worse, strained interpretations of the constitutional separation of church and state have in some cases produced overt government antagonism toward religion. The proper role for government is to support, not supplant, the involvement of religious institutions in their communities. Government can accomplish more by working with faith-based efforts than it can ever achieve by derailing them.

In Indianapolis, suburban and urban religious leaders regularly work with city officials to look for ways to reach out to communities in need. For example, in 1995 the city provided grants to twelve churches to run summer programs to develop skills, prevent violence, and provide evening recreation. Nearly 1,500 inner-city children participated. One of the churches runs a summer day camp in the park it maintains, and a local bank is setting up educational accounts for each camper.

Other faith-based groups provide assistance without the involvement of the city. The Care Center, for example, affiliated with the Englewood Christian Church, provides shelter to the homeless and victims of domestic violence, food and clothes to the destitute, and moral support to the poor in spirit. Before free, hot lunches are served at the center, a prayer is said. During the meal, a woman sings religious songs. The center furnishes medical and dental services and runs a camp program for children. In return, the center encourages (and in some cases requires) patrons to help on the grounds and attend religious services. Director Ernie Medcalfe says the Care Center is always in need of funding. The center could easily obtain a government grant—if it were willing to drop the religious component of its programs. But that, Ernie says, would eliminate the quality that makes the center successful.

The Salvation Army also combines assistance with religion in a way that profoundly affects the lives of many in need. Like the Care Center, the Salvation Army makes religious instruction and personal responsibility conditions of assistance. Every person housed in the group's Adult Rehabilitation Center must participate in religious services and work in some capacity for the good of the center. Work might include driving a truck, serving as a clerk, sorting through donated items that the center sells, or providing janitorial services. For the Salvation Army, there is a close connection between religious observance and self-sufficiency. As the director of the center expresses it, the Salvation Army believes that "if you make a man spiritually right, he can handle most of his problems on his own."

Twelve years ago, Becky Khan arrived at one of the organization's domestic violence shelters with three young children in tow. The shelter provided her with comfort, aid, support, and encouragement, and enrolled her in a support group for battered women. Becky often left the shelter through a back door that exited through a church, providing her first exposure to the Salvation Army's religious underpinnings. Slowly she became active in worship services. She later went on to earn her Graduate Equivalent Degree and become a teacher, and she now directs one of the organization's community facilities.

Other faith-based rehabilitation efforts show equally promising results. Consider the example of Teen Challenge, a worldwide Christian organization that helps people of all ages to escape from drug addiction. Studies have found that the group has long-term cure rates of 67 percent to 85 percent for drug addiction. These impressive results are achieved at a fraction of the cost of secular programs that have far lower success rates. Reverend Phil McClain, who directs Teen Challenge of Michigan, attributes this success to prayer and Bible study, noting that "[W]hen a student gets right with God, that is the starting point for progress."

Ironically, despite the success of programs like those run by the Salvation Army and Teen Challenge, these groups have at times met with government interference and antagonism. In an editorial for the *Wall Street Journal* (August 15, 1995) entitled "Addicted to Bureaucracy," Marvin Olasky describes how Texas bureaucrats opposed to the religious emphasis of the Teen Challenge program attempted to put them out of business. Good results were irrele-vant to state officials, who cited the program for not using state-licensed substance abuse coun-selors and proposed a fine of $4,000 a day.

> **Mayors of both parties have long known: The values associated with civility and reverence are far more essential to helping the inner cities than bigger government.**

The Salvation Army has also encountered government inter-ference, in this case from officials opposed to government support of faith-based nonprofit organizations. A decade ago a judge in Indianapolis prohibited the county government from providing homeless care through the Salvation Army because of its religious base. According to the judge, acceptance of government funds, amounting to 15 percent of the organization's revenues, required the cessation of mandatory church services in return for assis-tance.

Laws and regulations that prevent the government from using religious institutions to provide services have the ultimate if unin-tended effect of favoring homelessness over shelter with religion, and preferring addiction over treatment by unlicensed counselors. Significantly, these are all *voluntary* programs. Tragically, in some cases government aversion to religion is now so pronounced that bureaucrats actively discourage prayer and religious worship.

We experienced this firsthand in Indianapolis. Each year the federal government grants dollars to cities to fund summer jobs for youth. Although mayors appreciate the opportunity to be associated with any sort of job creation, the programs provide little lasting value. In the summer of 1994 we asked church groups to become involved in our job-training program in hopes that linkages would be created between underemployed urban youths looking for jobs and value-promoting institutions in their neighborhoods.

At the end of the summer the state of Indiana cited the city as "out of compliance" with a state law barring the use of funds for promoting religious activities. The state complained that participants voluntarily prayed before meals or going on field trips. Voluntary cursing, of course, did not create an offense, but voluntary praying violated the rules.

Every day, churches and faith-based organizations across America undertake extraordinary efforts to improve their communities and the lives of needy individuals. Many people are motivated by their faith to help the less fortunate. Faith works for a lot of people, and to the extent that government precludes groups from using this potent tool for positive change it does a great injustice.

Even simple cleanups can inspire confidence. A grandmother from out of town wrote me about her daughter, who lived with a fourteen-month-old baby in a difficult area. She writes of a visit after some storm damage when she "saw ten young people with rakes and shovels. They were cleaning our area of that debris! We asked and found out that they were from the International Church of God. Praise the Lord for such community service! They even invited us to their church and to an upcoming home-cooked dinner."

The issue is not partisan. While at a conference about juvenile crime, John Norquist, the bold Democratic mayor of Milwaukee, scribbled me a memorable note that read, "There are far greater threats to inner-city kids than religion." What the federal government has yet to figure out, mayors of both parties have long known: The values associated with civility and reverence are far more essential to helping the inner cities than bigger government.

Chapter Twelve

The Twenty-First Century City

In 1992 the nation's mayors greeted President Bill Clinton's arrival in Washington with glee. As their first order of business, they presented the new president with a "wish list" of more than five thousand construction projects in cities across the country. There was a feeling that big bucks were on the way from Congress, and the big-government, big-city mayors—who claimed that more money was all they needed to solve their problems—were pleased.

By 1997 the world had changed. Most of the big-city mayors who led the call for more federal dollars were gone, either through retirement or rejection by local electorates. In a national outcry for smaller government, voters took control of Congress away from the Democrats and presented it to the Republicans, who promptly began to shift authority to the local level. Even President Clinton nodded in the direction of smaller government, declaring that "the era of big government is over" as he signed important welfare reform legislation.

A new breed of mayors now occupies city halls across America. With a deep understanding of the need for smaller government, and determined to attain a better life for citizens in tough urban neighborhoods, these new mayors have blurred the lines between Republican and Democrat, conservative and liberal. They do not want bigger checks from Washington; they want the freedom to solve their cities' problems in their own way. In many respects, they have more in common with each other than they do with some of their respective parties' national leadership.

Democrats at the local level have concluded that big-government approaches to poverty do not work. These Democrat mayors realize that high taxes harm cities by driving out residents and businesses. Rather than increase his city's already high taxes, Philadelphia Mayor Ed Rendell took a watershed action in urban governance when he battled his public employee unions to reduce the cost of government. Milwaukee Mayor John Norquist, a self-proclaimed liberal when he served in the Wisconsin state legislature, became a passionate advocate of private school vouchers. Cleveland's Mike White stood up to old-style politicians and unions when he demanded that the provision of public services be opened up to competition. Mayor Richard Daley of Chicago, the home of patronage, changed the rules and allowed the private sector to participate in providing city services. Baltimore's Kurt Schmoke, in a remarkable action, not only gained control of the public schools, but also contracted with a private company to run some of them.

Republican mayors look different as well. Not long ago, Jack Kemp was the sole bleeding heart conservative, a lone voice in the Republican party preaching the importance of inner cities and opportunity for the poor. Beginning with Bret Shundler, who won an improbable election in overwhelmingly Democratic Jersey City by campaigning on school choice and small government, Republicans today occupy city halls across the country. Victories by Rudy Giuliani in New York and Richard Riordan in Los Angeles changed the political landscape of their cities, and proved that Republicans do have something to offer urban areas. Other dynamic new mayors, like Susan Golding in San Diego, are showing the way as well.

A new breed of mayors now occupies city halls across America.

These Republican mayors are acutely aware of their moral and economic responsibility to care about the residents of poor neighborhoods. Former prosecutor Rudy Giuliani did not fight crime by merely arresting more people. He embarked on a thoughtful campaign to fix broken windows, eradicate graffiti, evict the "squeegee men," and turn down the volume on boom boxes—thereby making the statement that poor neighborhoods should be safe, too.

In these pages I have attempted to describe a philosophy of government, an approach to urban neighborhoods, that can prepare America's cities to be successful in the twenty-first century. I owe an intellectual debt to all of these mayors. There is virtually nothing we have done in Indianapolis that has not already been tried someplace else. Because hundreds of elected officials and public managers from around the world have visited Indianapolis to learn from our initiatives, we in turn have had the opportunity to learn about the best government practices in this world.

We started with a clear and coherent philosophy of small government, incorporated good ideas, and put them into action. We have notched many successes, racked up some failures, and learned a great deal along the way.

The challenges facing America's cities are daunting. The prospect of exploding juvenile crime and teen pregnancy, along with failing public schools, is sobering. The mobility of wealth in the twenty-first century will prohibit mayors from raising taxes to fund even important services. "No new taxes" will be more than a political slogan—it will be an economic necessity. Yet I submit that the opportunity for positive change and progress in America's cities is greater today than at any time in the past thirty years.

> **The opportunity for positive change and progress in America's cities is greater today than at any time in the last thirty years.**

To do more with less, cities will increasingly explore the possibilities of competition and privatization. Unions will find that even Democratic city governments will no longer be the employer of last resort. These unions can become competitive, improving their pay and productivity in the process, or face real problems. Breaking up government monopolies will bring a new focus on outcomes, spawn innovation, and produce better services for customers.

Pressure from poor parents, civic leaders and even universities should eventually cause progressive state governments to authorize vouchers for children in urban districts. Increased funding for vouchers will force school boards, superintendents, and teachers' unions to allow more school-based decision making. In turn, teachers will insist that they be allowed to use their skill without the state legislature, school bureaucracy, or unions limiting their discretion.

The flaws of the welfare system are so profound and deeply entrenched that we are better off starting anew than attempting to reform the program. The best states will grant sweeping authority to local governments in order to promote creative and flexible solutions. Replacing the welfare bureaucracy with a competitive system of assistance will be essential to the future of our inner cities. Unemployed and working-poor adults will be able to choose among a variety of "intermediaries" who will compete for the opportunity to help them find and keep work. Some of these intermediaries will actually employ those who need help, managing their benefits and insurance and helping them develop long-term career opportunities.

By providing better services for less money, efficient, competitive city governments will have greater resources to dedicate to critical core services. The public depends on government to provide strong infrastructure,

Vibrant twenty-first century cities need just enough effective government, but can only succeed if healthy families instill positive values leading to opportunity and a good life.

and investing in this fundamental service can inspire confidence among urban citizens. Smooth streets and sidewalks and functioning sewer systems in even the poorest of neighborhoods send the important message to urban residents that the city cares about them and will support them.

Cities will not survive, let alone become great, unless they are safe. We must be prepared to invest heavily in public safety, but we also must change the way we police the city. Although implementation is difficult and old police cultures die slowly, good community policing works. Police will need the full support of their communities, the courts, and prison authorities to make our streets safe once again. The rising incidence, and ruthlessness, of juvenile crime will force the complete overhaul of the juvenile justice system in America. Inner-city residents will join with suburban conservatives in demanding a criminal justice system that works. As police effectively form relationships with neighbors, the newfound partners will demand better accountability from the judges and corrections authorities who allow revolving door justice.

No amount of government reform will save cities, however, without the support of active neighborhood-based organizations,

vibrant communities of faith, and strong families. Reducing government intrusion while increasing core services can help revitalize neighborhood leadership. Increasingly, public officials will give
community groups more authority over how services are delivered
in their areas. Good governments will end their aversion to religion and begin to support the efforts of faith-based groups and
promote their role in helping to bring the good and the virtuous
to our communities.

Too much government usurps the will of the community, but
ineffective government is harmful as well. The balance, good
and bad, was shown by a young man I met during a visit to
School 111. A twelve-year-old black male, whom we will call
William, ran up and gave me a hug—a quite unusual event for a
longtime prosecutor. I asked why. William said he now lived in a
safe house with a family who cared and a school that wanted him
to learn. He thanked me for the work of my wife, Margaret, who
is the supervisor of the truancy court.

That night Margaret told me about William's life in a house of
violence—neglected by a parent, ignored at school, and under the
influence of gangs. The child welfare authorities ignored his problems. Older gang members, unpunished by a permissive corrections system, sent William the message that their conduct was
acceptable. Then a committed school official called Margaret, and
eventually the court allowed William to be placed with the family
of a relative who cared for him and enrolled him in a school
with an attentive principal. The family and the school both
emphasized values and success. William began to flourish, physi-
cally and intellectually.

Vibrant twenty-first century cities achieve much of the same.
They need just enough effective government, but can only succeed
if healthy families instill positive values leading to opportunity
and a good life.

Wastewater Competition

As the largest city in America not located on a navigable body of water, Indianapolis has unique wastewater treatment needs. In order to meet these needs, the city employs two wastewater treatment plants located on the White River, a small river that runs through the heart of downtown Indianapolis. The first of these facilities, the Belmont plant, was constructed in 1924 and was continually upgraded and expanded thereafter in order keep up with the population, industrial, and commercial growth of the city. In 1966 the Southport plant was constructed nearby.

By 1982 these facilities had reached capacity. Both showed significant signs of decay and lacked the technology to meet the rigorous water standards established by the Clean Water Act of 1972 and other subsequent federal and state regulations. These stringent new standards required the plants to be capable of treating as many as 245 million gallons of wastewater a day while discharging their effluent into a very small body of water. Thus, with the help of the Environmental Protection Agency (EPA) and the state, the city upgraded the facilities to Advanced Wastewater Treatment plants (AWTs) through a massive, $250 million renovation that provided the plants with state-of-the-art equipment and dramatically improved their efficiency and capacity.

Over the next eleven years, the two plants won numerous accolades for innovation, safety, and overall outstanding performance. To many, the operations represented government at its best.

Although the plants were in good condition, the city's wastewater collection system was decaying badly. A 1991 report issued by the Indianapolis Chamber of Commerce entitled "Getting Indianapolis Fit for Tomorrow" identified more than $144 million worth of much-needed improvements to a long-neglected sewage collection system. In addition, the city had not raised sewer rates in over eight years. This combination put the City-County Council in the unenviable position of having to propose raising sewer usage rates by as much as 37 percent on approximately eight hundred thousand constituents.

At the same time, we knew that there were private companies across the United States and around the world that performed wastewater treatment. We considered even the rank of "best in class" to be somewhat meaningless, because comparisons could be drawn only with other government-run facilities.

If successful, putting the AWTs and/or their management into the marketplace promised us a high-profile opportunity to demonstrate the benefits of competition in providing city services.

Political Environment

Not surprisingly, there were a number of political obstacles to private involvement in running something so vital to the city's environment and the well-being of its citizens.

Environmental groups clamored about accountability and insisted that private management and concern for the environment could not coexist. Private managers, they argued, would cut corners and compromise environmental safety in order to maximize profits.

State and federal environmental regulators were not entirely enthusiastic, either. Many in the regional office of the EPA who participated in the planning and creation of these plants had concerns about private management. There was also some angst among members of Indiana's Department of Environmental Management and the Department of Natural Resources, many of whom tended to look upon private sector involvement as a criticism of their historic leadership and management.

Several members of the City-County Council also doubted the wisdom of private involvement in the administration of this critical function. Even within the corporate community there were concerns, with major generators of waste wanting to make certain that their rates were not raised and that existing pretreatment requirements were kept in place.

But the group most zealously opposed by far to outsourcing management of the plants was the local AFSCME Union. Employees were terrified of what the quest for reducing costs would mean to them. Cutting costs often means downsizing, and private companies with better technology would likely be less dependent upon manpower. Workers also suspected that even if they were retained, the need to maximize profits would yield lower salaries and reduced benefits.

There were also some interesting stakeholders that we failed to anticipate. Several of the local post-secondary educational institutions, many of which had both research and financial relationships with AWTs, had a stake in the outcome. Every supplier—from chemicals to toilet paper—wondered whether that relationship would be fractured by outsourcing. The sister union

at fleet services, which maintains city-owned vehicles, was concerned about where the vehicles used at the plant would be taken
for maintenance. The people who ran security at the plant wanted
to know whether they would be retained. All of a sudden, stakeholders we had not even considered came out of the woodwork
and became important voices in the debate. Communication
rapidly emerged as a critical element in executing the deal.

Examining the Options

In the spring of 1993 the city established a bipartisan review committee to examine the city's options, which included selling the
plants outright, maintaining city ownership and contracting out
operations, and maintaining city ownership and operation. The
review committee in turn hired the consulting firm of Ernst &
Young to evaluate operations at the plants, examine all options,
and recommend a course of action. Another firm, Camp, Dresser,
& McKee, was hired to perform a technical evaluation of the
plants.

Both studies concluded that the facilities were run effectively and efficiently and noted the many awards the plants had
received. The studies also observed that user fees had not
kept pace with costs, and recommended raising the fees in
order to reduce the need for other (property tax) dollars. Finally,
the studies found that the plants required significant capital
investments.

Ernst & Young predicted that contracting out management of
the plants would result in a mere 5 percent cost savings over opti-
mal city operation. Likewise, the firm concluded that plant staff
could be safely cut only by the same proportion.

So it was that our own consultants' study was used to club us
over the head. The Department of Public Works AFSCME

president, for example, took advantage of the situation by stand-
ing up in a council meeting and reading verbatim from the report
all the points that favored keeping the operation in-house.

Thus, although we believed that competition could produce
dramatically higher savings than our consultants predicted, pur-
suing the competitive process in the face of a report we ourselves
had commissioned was awkward, to say the least. But we were
still convinced that competition could improve any monopoly,
even if our AWTs were "best in class." We decided the most that
could be lost by putting the facilities into the competitive marketplace was a little bit of dignity and perhaps some political
capital. Had the marketplace verified that we were as good as
existing management claimed, we were prepared to celebrate
that success.

The Competitive Process

In May 1993 the city of Indianapolis distributed a Request for
Qualifications (RFQs) to a wide range of prospective providers.
The city sought companies with demonstrated experience in managing facilities of equal or greater complexity, world-class management talent and technological capability, a positive record of
working with employees at all levels and with unions in particular, and a strong record on environmental issues.

We indicated to the existing AWT management team that the
city would pay for legal, accounting, and management consulting
teams of their choosing. Union workers had the option of joining
the city managers in their bid, but opted not to for several reasons.
Relations at the plant between city managers and union workers
were not good, and union leadership did not expect management
to trim the bureaucratic bloat to the extent necessary to compete
against private proposals. Union leaders also made a strategic

decision to forgo participation so that if necessary they could block the competition by staging a public fight.

We received qualification submissions from some of the largest and best private operators in the world. Of the seven companies that sought to participate in the process, we asked five for proposals.

The Request for Proposals

Several critical issues required careful consideration, the most obvious and important of which was that of control. Members of the City-County Council were loathe to have their control over plant operations diminished and worried about a lack of responsiveness and accountability from private management. Beyond that, councilors, environmental groups, and the public at large worried that the profit motive would undermine safety or adversely affect rates.

Policy-making authority needed to remain in the hands of city government. Rates would continue to be determined by members of the City-County Council.

We insisted that the new management meet or exceed previous environmental standards. In the past, the plants had always discharged effluent far cleaner than required by EPA regulations, and now many worried that private management would allow environmental quality to deteriorate right up to the edge of those standards in order to cut costs.

One of the compromises we had to make for not selling the plants altogether was paying for capital investments. Prior to contracting out the plants, the city put together a list of $22 million in capital improvements the internal engineers viewed as necessary. An outright sale of the plants would have relieved the city of the responsibility for making the capital investments. However, tax laws, federal repayment options, and anxiety about the transaction limited the management contract to five years. City responsibility for capital investments also had its detractors: opponents of the deal predicted that such an arrangement would prompt vendors to increase their capital spending in order to decrease their maintenance obligations.

We decided that the city would continue to pay for the capital investments while holding management responsible for preventive maintenance, with a series of thresholds in the contract for what constituted capital and noncapital items.

The Response

Any nervousness we felt following our consultant's report evaporated when the city received its responses. Astonishingly, the proposal entered by our own in-house team—which only weeks before insisted that $30 million a year was the absolute minimum amount required to run the plant—reduced that price by 10 percent when subjected to competition.

The eventual winner, the White River Environmental Partnership (WREP), included Suez Lyonnaise des Eaux, a French partner that is one of the largest providers of wastewater treatment in the world, JMM Operational Services, Inc., a Denver-based company with an impeccable reputation for environmental safety, and a controlling interest by the private Indianapolis Water Company.

WREP promised to cut costs by 40 percent, reduce the work force at the plant by 37 percent, and save the city $65 million over five years while matching or exceeding the previous environmental performance.

Unlike the city managers, the private firm guaranteed results. If city management fell short of the savings they promised, they could be fired, but that would be of little value to the city and its taxpayers. The private companies, on the other hand, had enormous assets to back their promises.

The private vendor would take full responsibility of meeting all existing federal, state, and local requirements.

As for capital investments, WREP stunned us by coming back with capital plans smaller than our own. Rather than inflating their estimated capital needs, the private proposals actually promised to reduce our capital needs and at the same time assume responsibility for all maintenance obligations.

While WREP agreed to pay comparable wages and benefits, union leadership was taken aback by the reductions in work force. Of the 321 workers, WREP wished to retain fewer than 200. In response, the union reverted to a more traditional, adversarial approach to privatization, mounting a highly visible campaign in the media, meeting regularly with members of the City-County Council, and forming coalitions with environmental groups and others opposed to the outsourcing. The union also filed a lawsuit against the city, and sought political intervention in Washington, DC, with the EPA.

Transition

Although the wastewater treatment aspect of the transition from public to private management went off without a hitch, the personnel side was a bit more complicated. Although WREP agreed to accept and recognize the union, tough issues remained.

Under the agreement, WREP was required to interview every existing worker, but was not obligated to hire anyone. Any worker who refused an offer from WREP of a comparable job (with comparable defined as +/–1 pay grade) was on his own. Of the 321 existing AWT employees, WREP hired 196. At that point, the city, the union, and WREP came together to design the "safety net" employment agreement.

Those not hired by WREP were offered a choice of a job with the city in another department or a severance package. About half of these workers opted for the severance package, which included employment counseling and out-placement help, while the other half entered the safety net. Under the program, fifty employees not hired at WREP would be utilized on specific city projects until regular union jobs opened through attrition.

Months earlier, we anticipated a workforce reduction at the AWT plants and began banking vacancies at the city to help absorb displaced workers. The city offered workers union jobs within the city as they became available on the basis of seniority. For example, former AWT employees, already familiar with the sewer system, maintained sewer lines while awaiting a permanent position elsewhere in city government. Within a year all safety net workers had been placed.

Results

Two years into the contract, the cost savings to the city realized by private management exceeded initial projections, totaling $22.6 million. WREP made specific reductions in utility costs (reduced by 20 percent), corrective maintenance costs (down 30 percent), and unanticipated capital expenditures (down 20 percent). With respect to capital investments, WREP's attention to preventive maintenance increased the reliability of the city's equipment, resulting in fewer breakdowns and more dependable operation. Proposed savings on capital expenditures surpassed initial estimates for an additional $4.2 million in savings over the five-year contract. The city also received $57,010 in energy rebates from the Indianapolis Power and Light Company in recognition of the energy efficient motors designed and installed by WREP personnel. WREP decreased the number of effluent violations by more than 50 percent compared to prior city operations, even as maximum flows hover some 27 percent above peak design capacity.

One of the efficiencies WREP realized is a dramatic improvement in the time it takes to process invoices to vendors. According to a Dun & Bradstreet review (February, 1996), WREP ranked in the top 1 percent of companies for providing on-time payment within terms. Prompt processing provides opportunities for small businesses that cannot endure the capital strain of government purchasing, and creates pricing advantages from vendors who do not have to build interest mark-ups into their price quotes to secure business.

Minority- and women-owned businesses greatly benefited. In 1995, 22.7 percent of WREP purchases were made from minority-owned or women-owned firms—well above the targeted 12 percent rate and worth recognition by both the Indianapolis Black Chamber of Commerce and the Indiana Regional Minority Supplier Development Council.

In addition, WREP can take those minority firms into new markets. The city, for example, cannot partner with a small local firm and help it enter a new market in Chicago. But the partners that comprise WREP can create opportunities for minority businesses in other communities.

Accountability

Government's control today is greater than ever—the quality and volume of the data are far beyond anything ever generated under previous management. And the participation of the environmental community in our daily operations has been greatly enhanced. WREP created the AWT Advisory Group, comprised of independent industry experts and environmentalists, which meets monthly to review the operation of the plants and advise the city on long-term needs and planning activities.

Work Force

The existing work force receives higher salaries, better benefits, and more training. As of 1996 WREP employees' raises and bonuses averaged 4.1 percent increases, compared to the 2.65 percent guaranteed for city union employees. Over the two-year period in discussion, 1994 to 1996, WREP workers earned an average of 4.89 percent more than they had in their former city positions. And union grievances decreased from the previous average of thirty-eight per year under city management to one in 1994 and zero in 1995.

While the accident rate decreased 70 percent in the first year of the contract, second-year figures show an additional 42 percent decrease, demonstrating an overall 80 percent reduction in the number of accidents per year. The decline in accidents also resulted in a 91 percent reduction in lost work days and a 60 percent reduction in restricted duty limitations. Increased plant safety performance resulted in a tangible 8 percent reduction in workers' compensation insurance rates for the company.

Conclusions

Not surprisingly, the eighteen-month–long process of contracting out the AWT facilities was too fast for many. For others, despite the numerous public meetings and extensive television, radio, and newspaper coverage, the process was not sufficiently public. In the end, the criticism that we could have done more was impossible to avoid and we were left struggling to find a reasonable balance between talking and doing.

In putting AWT operations into the marketplace, we learned several valuable lessons that we have attempted to incorporate into subsequent competitive efforts. For example, the privatization of the AWTs marked the first time the city brought in legislators early in a competitive effort.

We also learned that it was impossible to overcommunicate with stakeholders, the council, and the general public on these issues and that, despite the extraordinary amount of time it required, daily communication with most stakeholders was essential to moving the process along.

The disparity between the consultant's cost savings estimates and those realized by vendors led us to reexamine the role we asked consultants to play in the competitive process. We determined that there was little point in hiring a consultant to tell us how much a vendor would charge to provide a given service. A more appropriate role for the consulting firms, we discovered, was to have them assist in analyzing the proposals entered by vendors and in ascertaining whether those proposals were realistic, based on the quality and price of service those vendors were providing at other locations.

Politically, the success of the privatization of the AWTs helped lend credibility to our competitive approach, but beyond that it produced relatively few direct benefits. The $65 million savings, though, did allow us to avoid the proposed sewer user rate increase, and produced additional dollars for our infrastructure rebuilding program.

Privatizing operations of two exceedingly well-run facilities— and improving environmental quality and saving millions in the process—says something important about government benchmarks: If you want to find out how well government is providing a given service, do not compare yourself only to other government providers, but to the entire market—public and private, domestic and international. Especially where government is concerned, "best in class" and "best in the world" are two quite different concepts, and there is no reason public officials and citizens should settle for the former when the latter is readily available.

Airport Competition

A well-run airport can be a great asset for a city's economic development efforts. Airports have increasingly become centers of intermodal transportation—a combination of trucking, rail, and air—and thus an important means of distributing goods.

Indianapolis International Airport is particularly suited to become a leading distribution hub because of the city's central location and excellent access to highways. In the 1990s Indianapolis International beat tough competition to secure an $800 million United Airlines maintenance facility, a $350 million Federal Express hub, and a $60 million United States postal hub. The airport's passenger count more than doubled from 1984 to 1994.

Yet despite these successes, there were challenges on the horizon. The airport's cost per passenger was rising fast, up 38 percent in the last ten years. Revenue from concessions remained flat, even while the airport industry as a whole was enjoying substantial growth in such revenue. Finally, the airport faced significant capital needs—within ten to fifteen years, the airport would have to build a new terminal.

The airport is managed by the Indianapolis Airport Authority, an independent municipal corporation established to maintain, operate, and finance airport facilities within and surrounding Indianapolis. The airport authority is governed by a seven-member board, five of whom are appointed by the mayor. As a municipal corporation, the authority has the ability to issue debt and to levy taxes independently of other government entities. While the authority issues debt to fund capital improvements, land acquisition, and other long-term projects, it has never used its taxing authority.

Airlines that operate out of Indianapolis International do so under a contractual agreement with the airport, known as a Residual Lease Agreement, which shifts the risk associated with operating revenue shortfalls directly to the airlines. To oversimplify, airport officials add up their expenses, subtract revenues from parking, concessions, and other non-airline earnings, and charge the difference to airlines. The agreement protects taxpayers, but also provides no incentives for the airport authority to operate efficiently, since rising costs are simply passed along to the airlines. Not surprisingly, airport charges are the fastest growing component of airline operating costs—accounting for 5 percent of their total costs. If we wanted to establish Indianapolis International Airport as the premier distribution hub in North America, we needed to change the equation and create incentives to operate efficiently.

Examining the Options

In the summer of 1994, the airport authority created the Managed Competition Committee to oversee a competitive initiative.

Although selling the airport outright was an attractive option in many ways, it was not one we considered very seriously. While a sale would eliminate future capital obligations and generate substantial immediate revenue, our experience in previous years with trying to get approval for asset sales was not encouraging. We also wanted all policy-making authority to remain with the public airport board. Thus, we decided to maintain ownership but contract out management of some or all airport operations.

The group with which we had to be most careful were the airlines, which are formidable and substantial private enterprises. Many airlines were concerned that the goal of competing-out airport management was to generate savings that could be siphoned away from the airport and used for other municipal expenses. Approval from the airlines was important to a successful contract, so it was essential for us to assure the airlines that they would be the primary beneficiaries of any savings generated from outsourcing.

While taxpayers would not benefit directly from any savings, they would benefit, we hoped, from better airport service and additional economic development at the airport.

The Competitive Process

The first step was a Request for Qualifications from companies interested in submitting proposals. The result was encouraging, as we received responses from some of the world's premier airport operators. The existing airport management team decided to compete as well, an occurrence that had become commonplace in our experience with competition.

We asked five prospective vendors, including the existing management team, to submit proposals that would meet four goals. First, we wanted their best ideas for providing improved service at the same or lower cost. Second, we wanted their ideas for attracting new economic development at the airport. Third, we wanted long-term plans for positioning the airport in the twenty-first century. Finally, we asked them how they would increase the expertise and diversity of the airport staff.

As in the case of our wastewater treatment plants, we knew capital improvements were going to be a challenging issue. Because the airport authority operated on a five-year capital budget, we had a feel for the capital work that was going to be needed. The major capital project was an enormous one—the new terminal. To the extent that we could get a private manager to contribute to that project in a cost-effective manner, it would benefit the airlines as well as the airport authority.

The Proposals

The five proposals offered a series of brilliant suggestions. One proposal suggested that the airport drop its plan to build a new terminal, redesign the existing terminals, and use the land for commercial development instead. Another proposed using part of the airport's real estate for a golf course. Although the existing management team submitted an excellent proposal with substantial improvements over previous operations, it could not match the resources and creativity of the private vendors. One of the biggest problems was that the public employees could not guarantee the savings in their proposal like the private vendors could.

We narrowed the field to two finalists, both of whom proposed a management fee that included a fixed annual payment and an incentive payment based on performance. During final negotiations, both eliminated the fixed annual payment and agreed to be paid on performance alone.

After a thorough evaluation process, the airport authority signed a ten-year contract with BAA USA, the American subsidiary of a British company that manages seven airports overseas, handling more than eighty million passengers annually. Interestingly, BAA is the product of privatization—it is the former British Airport Authority, converted to private ownership by Margaret Thatcher in 1987. Today, BAA has more than $3.7 billion in shareholders' equity and fixed assets of more than $5 billion. In the United States, BAA has implemented many of its retailing and management principles at the successful AirMall located at the Greater Pittsburgh International Airport.

The airport authority selected BAA due to its:

- Strong record of success in similar airports;
- Substantial corporate resources and excellent financial performance over the past ten years;
- Commitment to customer service; and
- Long-term vision and approach

BAA identified cost savings and non-airline revenue increases totaling more than $100 million over the ten years of the contract. The contract guarantees savings of $32 million, and the company is not paid until after it saves $3.2 million each year. The company even posted a $50 million letter of credit to back its guarantee. BAA and the airport authority share all savings beyond the contract price, with the airport authority receiving 60 percent in the first year, 65 percent in the second, and 70 percent thereafter.

These savings are not the product of wholesale employee layoffs and salary cuts. In fact, BAA hired all of the existing airport employees, and at comparable wages and benefits. Instead, BAA relies on innovative management to improve airport operations. The company plans to increase airport revenue by aggressively courting new retail shops and developing new and better services for airport customers. It plans to bring down operating costs by drawing on its superior worldwide expertise and bringing the best technology and the best management practices to our airport. Most important, BAA does not get paid unless it succeeds in these endeavors.

Other contract provisions include an agreement by BAA to contract extensively with minority- and women-owned businesses. BAA also implemented its "street pricing" approach to concessions, dictating that prices for goods sold within the airport are comparable to the rates in the area as a whole. Indianapolis travelers also benefit from a provision that requires BAA to develop a Quality Service Monitor program to assess the attitude and helpfulness of the staff, airport cleanliness, crowding, and other factors that affect travelers.

The Benefits of Competition

Today, the airport authority remains responsible for long-range planning and strategic decision-making and continues to make decisions on capital expenditures, oversee debt, assure compliance with federal regulations, and monitor BAA's performance.

More than a year into the contract, BAA reduced the airport's cost per passenger from an average of $6.70 in 1994 to $3.87 in 1996. Concession and parking revenue per passenger has increased by 50%, from $2.14 in 1994 to $3.32 in 1996. As a result, BAA reduced airline landing fees at Indianapolis International by 70%, saving the fourteen airlines that regularly operate at the airport $7 million during BAA's first fifteen months of management.

The resulting lower airline fees should have a ripple effect that benefits the airline industry, the city, and the consumer. Taxpayers will benefit from lower airport costs because Indianapolis' low fees and professional approach will be a magnet for increased economic activity. New maintenance facilities, air-cargo traffic, and airline routes are all rational expectations.

Local customers will certainly notice an increase in service. Instead of viewing an airline traveler as a captive audience for overpriced goods and services—a very government way of looking at things—BAA negotiates with its tenants to provide an expanded range of retail and street pricing. BAA's philosophy is that airline travelers should pay the same price for a pack of gum at the airport that they pay at the corner drug store. Airport passengers may even notice a decrease in airfare as the number of airline routes increases.

Naval Air Warfare Center

The Naval Air Warfare Center is a 163-acre military facility that designs and produces advanced electronics and aviation equipment for aircraft, ships, satellites, and other military vessels. NAWC, as it is called, has been one of the least costly, highest quality facilities of its type since it opened in 1942. It is the only military installation in the country with the flexibility to conceive, design, prototype, and manufacture avionics and electronic equipment on site. Among NAWC's contributions to America's defense were the Norden Bombsight used in World War II for high-altitude bombing, and technology for the weapons guidance systems that American pilots used during the Persian Gulf War.

NAWC also happens to be one of the largest employers in Indianapolis. The base employs 2,400 people at an average salary that exceeds $45,000. NAWC's contribution to the local economy is estimated at one billion dollars. So when the federal government started plans to close dozens of military bases across the country, we were understandably concerned.

Losing NAWC would be an enormous blow to the Indianapolis economy. Although NAWC survived the first round of cuts in 1991, we were less optimistic about our chances in later rounds. We started planning a response before NAWC wound up on the closure list.

Examining the Options

Our early efforts included several ideas for changing NAWC's role within the nation's defense structure. One option was to capitalize on Indianapolis' emerging status as a national air freight and distribution hub, and turn the base into an international distribution center for the military.

A second option was to assume that shrinking defense budgets would require the Navy to increase its outsourcing of electronics. In this scenario, the experts at NAWC could be "smart buyers" of equipment in the increasingly complex and fast-changing electronics industry.

A third option was to consolidate several NAWC functions with Navy bases in nearby Bloomington, Indiana, and Louisville, Kentucky. A study in the summer of 1994 found that the federal government could save $50 million annually through such a realignment, without closing any of the three sites.

We shopped these ideas inside the Pentagon for months, but found little enthusiasm and no internal champions. The Department of Defense had established a very strict methodology for closing bases, and those responsible for the closing viewed our suggestions as complications, not useful alternatives. Many officials also feared setting any kind of precedent that would undermine base closings elsewhere.

Although Indiana was fortunate to have several influential representatives in Washington, history suggested that no amount of political lobbying would save the base either. We realized there was no way NAWC would stay open as a government military base.

Pursuing Privatization

In 1994 we met with Navy officials to discuss a fourth alternative to closing the NAWC facilities: privatization. We would spin off NAWC as a private company, and sell its services back to the military. Our experiences in other areas gave us confidence that privatization could offer the Navy the best of both worlds: it could meet the goals of closing a base and reducing costs, while still retaining access to the expertise that had accumulated at NAWC.

We found considerable resistance to the idea among many military officials, who felt that closure was the only workable solution. Even more frustrating, the Navy indicated that any thoughts of restructuring would have to wait until after the base had been closed—a task we knew would be far more difficult than selling a fully operational facility.

We entered a holding pattern with the Navy, but continued to develop our plans for privatization. We created a team consisting of the Hudson Institute and Arthur Andersen to prepare for what seemed inevitable.

On February 28, 1995, our fears were realized. The Base Realignment and Closure Commission released its recommendation of facilities to be shut down in the third wave of base closings, and NAWC was on the list. Our team immediately began to examine the commission's recommendation and prepare an alternative proposal.

When the commission held its public hearing on the closure in the summer of 1995, we were ready. Instead of joining the chorus of those who wanted to prevent closure of their local base, we took a different approach. We simply asked that if the federal government closed NAWC, it do so in a logical way. We submitted a privatization plan that made more economic and military sense than shutting down the facility. The proposal met the Pentagon's downsizing goals, avoided the estimated $180 million cost of closing the base, and retained NAWC as a military resource. The competitive process was a no-lose proposition for the federal government, because if it did not like the result, it could close the base as planned.

The plan contained three basic elements:

- NAWC would be closed as a military base, with a corresponding reduction in the number of government employees.
- The city would assume ownership of the site, facilities, and equipment and would be responsible for operating and maintenance costs.
- One or more private companies—to be established on the site—would perform work under contract to the military.

Initially, the new firms would provide products and services under the auspices of a sole-source agreement with the Defense Department, providing a seamless transition. In five years or less, the firms would have to compete for defense contracts.

By offering to take ownership of the facility during the transition, and thereby shift the risk of failure from the Navy to the city, we were able to convince the commission to give privatization a chance. Although we did not convince the commission to choose privatization as a substitute for closure, the commission did specifically identify privatization as an option the Navy could pursue in conjunction with closing the base. In his letter submitting the closure list to Congress, President Clinton lent his strong support for privatization and encouraged the Navy to take a much closer look at the Indianapolis proposal.

Privatization would be given a chance. Now our task was to demonstrate that the strategy would provide greater benefit to the Navy than the traditional closing procedure. This was new territory for us, the Navy, and private companies, and there was no way for us to be certain that private companies would even be interested in such a deal. That was for the marketplace to decide.

Making Privatization Work

In August 1995 the city established the Reuse Planning Authority to manage the privatization and base closure processes. The nine-member board included representatives from the City-County Council, the school board, and prominent local executives. The base's commanding officer and others participated on a nonvoting basis.

We requested and received senior management support from four local companies to assist in formulating the city's strategy for privatization. In particular Joe Doyle, the chief financial officer of Allison Engine-Rolls Royce, helped us structure our Request for Proposals and evaluate responses.

One of the first steps was to determine the true cost of the closure option. We found that the Navy's financial model was a real estate model that looked at operating costs that could be avoided, similar to cost savings from consolidating two manufacturing plants. In the case of NAWC, however, the value of the base lay more in the knowledge of its employees than in the cost of its equipment. We wanted the Navy to understand the value of losing the expertise at NAWC.

An employee survey in the fall of 1995 found that only 26 percent of NAWC employees were willing to move in order to stay with the Navy. The remaining 74 percent preferred getting private sector jobs in Indianapolis. This survey had important implications for the close-and-move alternative because it implied significant program disruptions and losses in the Navy's core avionics competencies. Other Navy closing sites were experiencing drastic losses in experienced personnel due to people's unwillingness to move after closure, and the Navy was becoming sensitive to this issue.

The disruption to the Navy's technology, the high up-front cost of closing, the President's approval, and the city's enthusiasm began to tip the scales in favor of privatization. The critical piece was a leader inside the Defense Department to champion the idea. We found that leader in Vice Admiral John Lockard, the recently appointed commander of the Naval Air Systems Command. Lockard displayed remarkable vision and flexibility, agreeing not only that NAWC should be privatized, but that the city should manage the competition for a private company (or companies) to take over the facility.

Allowing the city to manage the process had two very important consequences. First, it meant that the Navy took a large step, perhaps inadvertently, in thinking of itself as a customer. Second, it meant the process could move quickly, unencumbered by federal restrictions that bogged down virtually all other large federal privatizations.

The Proposals

Instead of dictating how privatization was to be accomplished, we identified a few broad goals and allowed the respondents to come up with creative solutions for achieving them. The Request for Proposals was only seventeen pages long. Our primary goals were to balance the interests of the four major stakeholders so that all realized their own objectives. The desired outcomes for each major stakeholder were:

Employees: New job opportunities and employment growth

Navy: Cost, quality, and performance enhancements

Business entity: Long-term profitable growth

Community: Economic development, a technology spur, a new tax base, and a long-term commitment from the business entity

Although we received seven excellent proposals, none matched the one submitted by Hughes Technical Services Company, Inc., a subsidiary of Hughes Electronics. Hughes' reputation, its relationship with the Navy, its progressive employee relations, and its competitive pricing combined to give the company the edge.

Hughes agreed to employ almost all existing workers when it took over NAWC and to increase its local employment to at least three thousand by the year 2002. Workers would receive the same or better wages and benefits than they had with the Navy.

Hughes will pay an estimated $3 million in property taxes to the city—which previously received no tax revenues from the base—and will be responsible for all maintenance and utility costs at the site. Hughes has also pledged to invest more than $200 million in employee training, applied research, and capital improvements to the facility.

On September 25, 1996, the Navy signed a one-year contract with Hughes, retaining four additional one-year options. The contract enables NAWC's customers to enjoy a smooth transition in

the fulfillment of their workload contracts while the facility pre-
pares to compete for Navy business within the next five years. The
workload contract allows the entire United States government,
not merely the Navy, to place orders with the facility.

By saving the Navy the expense of closing the base and by producing equipment more cost-effectively, privatization will save the
federal government an estimated $1 billion over ten years.

The Navy now leases NAWC's facilities and equipment to the
city of Indianapolis, and the city subleases them to Hughes. Both
leases are for $1 a year, last for ten years with two five-year
options, and recognize that Hughes will gain title to the facility
(and to the equipment at the facility) as soon as the city gains title
from the Navy. The city retains the right to develop unimproved
land at the site that Hughes is not using.

Conclusions

The unprecedented agreement among the Navy, Hughes, and Indianapolis presents a twenty-first century vision of how the defense
establishment can be reinvented. The agreement between Hughes
and the Navy is not merely contractual, but creates a relationship
that increases flexibility, reduces costs, and uses private sector
expertise in providing goods and services to meet our defense
needs.

Under privatization, each party to the transaction comes out a
winner. The Navy will reduce personnel, save considerable
amounts of money, and close a base while retaining access to
world-class electronics expertise. NAWC's employees will keep or
increase their pay and benefits and have greater job opportunities
with Hughes. Hughes will take over a successful operation that
has enormous potential in a growing market and that is stafffed

with highly experienced workers. The city will preserve jobs and create new ones, put a new entity on the property tax rolls, and further its edge in the field of advanced electronics. All this occurred because the artificial barrier between public and private was removed—replaced by innovative and profitable solutions.

Index